MAKIN' THINGS©
for kids

By Ed and Stevie Baldwin

Dorison House Publishers, Boston

ACKNOWLEDGMENTS

We wish to acknowledge the assistance and support of the following people, without whose help "Makin' Things" would not have happened:

Denny Allen, Allen Bragdon, Jane Croll, Joe Hardt, Bob Haring, Nancy Jackson, and Jon Petre.

Also to our parents, John and Annabelle Thompson and Art and Dorothy Baldwin, whose moral support helped us through all the bleak years.

And especially to Jack Sheehan who said, "You can be anything you want to be in America with hard work, patience and perseverance."

Finally, we are grateful to the numerous editors for their suggestions and encouragement.

Copyright © The Family Workshop, Inc.

Published by Dorison House Publishers, Inc.
824 Park Square Building, Boston, Massachusetts 02116

ISBN: 916752—33—x

Library of Congress Catalog Card Number: 78-73845

Manufactured in the United States of America

CONTENTS

FOREWORD

Ed and Stevie (Stephanie) Baldwin have 5 children and have produced these projects for their own children's use. Their own little consultants have personally road tested these toys to iron out all the kinks. Make your own adaptations or changes or personalize a toy for your favorite child and enjoy the delight when they warmly respond to your efforts.

These are a small collection of the many children's projects seen in the Baldwin's nationally syndicated newspaper columns, "Makin' Things" and "Kids Stuff." Watch for them in your local newspaper.

Before attempting to build any of the projects in the book, be certain to review and understand each step of construction and to verify all of the dimensions. While every effort has been made to ensure accuracy in these designs and drawings, the possibility of error always exists and the publisher cannot accept responsibility for materials improperly used or designs not first verified.

TOY BUILDING TIPS & TECHNIQUES

We have found that perfection in toy making is not really necessary. The fact that a wheel is not quite round or a paint job not as good as it could be doesn't matter. The recipient is going to be more interested in the function than the flaws. The fact that you took the time to make it in the first place is the important point.

It is essential, however, to construct toys so that they will not harm the intended user. Some good rule of thumb items to remember in toy construction are:

- always glue wood joints
- use screws instead of nails where possible
- always sand the edges of plywood
- seal the finished toy in a non-toxic paint or varnish
- carefully instruct the child how the toy should be used

Toys from found materials

Many of the toys in this book can be made from scrap lumber and odds and ends from around the house. As an example, empty milk cartons can be covered with paper and turned into little houses. The plastic milk cartons can be cut up and made into plastic washers to use for making wheels run smoothly on little cars.

Visit construction sites where new homes are being built. Many contractors will be more than glad to have you haul off the scraps. Tin cans when painted will make great headlights on the Super Car.

Pointers on tools (some you can make)

If you are lucky enough to have a complete workshop, then read no further. If you have to make do with a few hand tools, take heart! There are several things you can do that are very inexpensive and yet are very helpful.

One of the least expensive ways to add tools to

your collection is to shop garage sales. Look for small classified ads in the local newspapers. Every town has someone who buys and sells used tools; look for that person in your town. Look for bargain tool sales. Sears and other stores will refurbish tools that were returned, and resell them at substantial savings. If you are really determined to get some big power tools, take a careful look at multipurpose tools before buying a table saw, drill press, and lathe.

Some companies make multipurpose tools that combine many tool features for less money than each unit would cost if bought separately. If you're looking into table saws, do buy a table saw before you buy a radial arm saw. A radial is a dangerous saw. A table saw can do more, is more accurate, and is safer.

You can take old washing machine and dryer motors and mount them on your workbench and buy attachments such as sanding drums, etc. that are very useful and inexpensive.

Some multipurpose tools can combine many functions for less money than individual units purchased separately. This tool can saw, sand, drill, rout, and can be used as a lathe.

Finishing tips

Always use non-toxic paints on toys. Most lead paints are now off the market so your selection will be limited to acrylic latex, spray acrylics and lacquers, some oil-based alkyds, and polyurethanes.

If you buy a good brand of acrylic latex exterior trim enamel you will get a fast-drying paint that will last practically forever, covers in 1 coat, and dries with no brush marks. Most canned spray paints do not cover in 1 coat and generally are more expensive than the kind you brush on. For clear finishes that last, polyurethane is good. We usually use 2 coats on surfaces such as play tables and chairs.

Getting toys to stay in one piece

Making toys stay put together can be quite a job. We have 5 children, and sometimes even the 1 toy we've proclaimed unbreakable gets demolished. Generally speaking, if you use the right fasteners and glues you can avoid any immediate breakdowns. Use screws wherever possible instead of nails. Recess the screw heads to avoid scratches on little bodies.

The 2 glues we use exclusively are aliphatic resin (a cream-colored glue) sold as carpenter's glue for inside projects. For toys to be used out of doors we use clear epoxy. It fills poorly cut joints, is waterproof, and holds quite well. Always clamp glue joints and always use nails or screws in conjunction with glue.

For gluing laminates such as formica or veneer, use white-colored acrylic latex contact cement.

Enlarging scale patterns

Obviously it is difficult to have full size patterns in a book. It is easy, however, to enlarge scale patterns and keep the design in proportion as you increase its size. This is easily done. Here's how: if the grid for your pattern is ¼-inch scale = 2 inches, you draw 2-inch squares on the board (or tracing paper if the material is fabric). Then transfer the design from the small pattern to the larger surface, working each small square to the corresponding large square.

You can make even smaller blocks by tracing the original design and dividing the squares into triangles as shown. This will make it easier to transfer the design by giving you smaller sections of the pattern to deal with. You can also buy "to scale" graph paper, transfer the design to full size, then trace it onto the material using carbon paper.

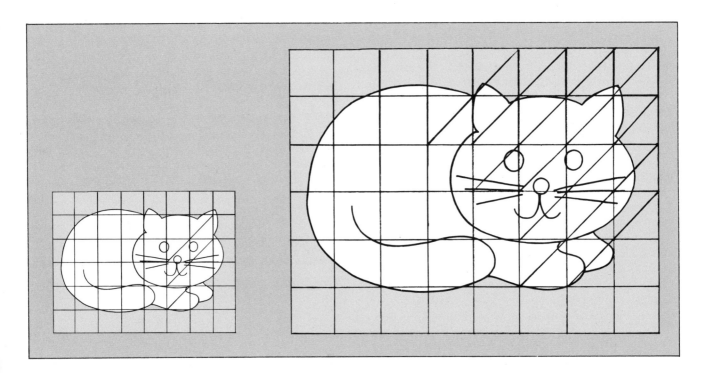

ROCKING HORSE

Materials

¾ -in. diameter wooden dowel rod, 8-in. long
1 × 12 white pine lumber (or equivalent),
    8 ft. long
4 finishing nails, 2½-in. long
14 wood screws, 1½-in. long, (thin gauge)
4 sheets of garnet sandpaper; 2 rough and
    2 medium
Wood filler (optional) to cover nail holes

Tools

Screwdriver (to match the size of the screw head).
Nailset to recess nails (a large nail will substitute).
Drill with ¾-in. (spade) drill bit, and a bit slightly
   smaller than the diameter of the wood screws.
Router with corner-round bit (optional).
Sabre saw (or coping saw), ruler, and hammer.

Cutting, drilling and sanding

1. There are 6 cutting pieces: head (A) rocker support (B), center support (C), rocker (D), seat (E), and backrest (F).

2. Enlarge the scale pattern pieces. Directions for enlarging and transferring the full-size patterns to wood are given under "Toy Building Tips and Techniques" at the beginning of the book.

3. Cut carefully along the outline of each pattern piece using a sabre saw (or coping saw). A suggested layout for pattern pieces is given in Figure A.

4. Drill a ¾-in.-diameter hole through the head piece where indicated on the pattern. This will accommodate the wooden dowel rod handle which will be added later.
   An optional step at this point is to use a router to round all edges of the rockers and seat, the edges of the head (excluding the bottom), the curved sides of the rocker supports, and the top and sides of the backrest.

5. Carefully sand the cut edges of all pieces, first with coarse sandpaper and then with medium to remove any splinters or rough edges that might hurt little ones.

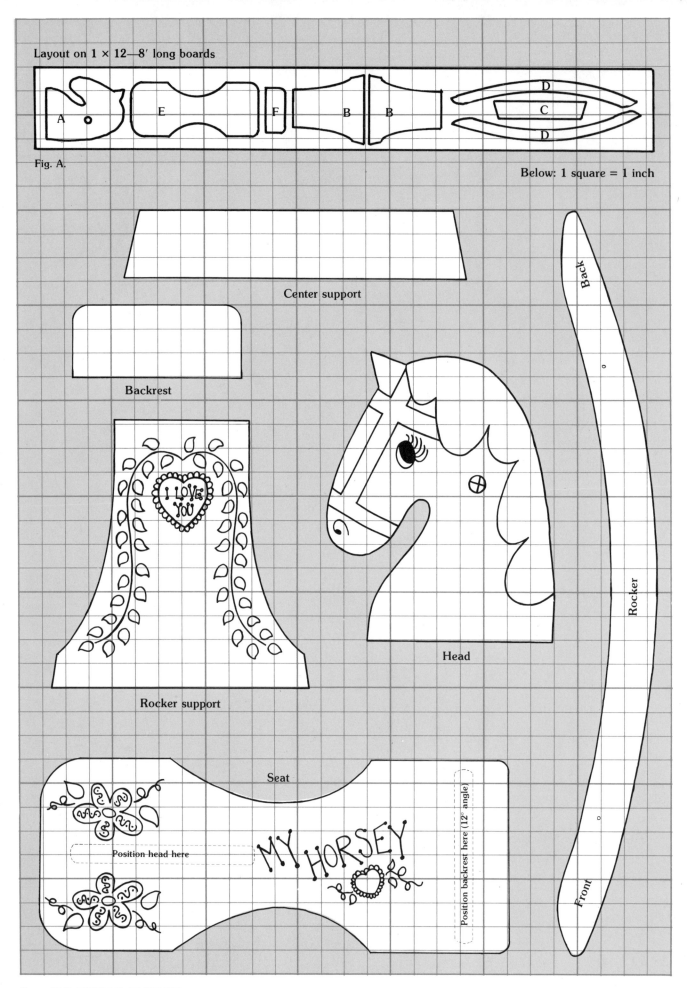

Layout on 1 × 12—8′ long boards

A · E · F · B · B · D · C · D

Fig. A.

Below: 1 square = 1 inch

Center support

Backrest

Back

Rocker

Rocker support

Head

I LOVE YOU

Seat

Position head here

Position backrest here (12° angle)

MY HORSEY

Front

Assembling

1. Carefully center each of the rocker supports at the top edges of the center support as shown in Figure B. Drill holes for 4 screws (2 on each side) and fasten the pieces together.

2. Notice that the narrow end of the rocker supports extends above the top of the center support (Figure C). Trim the tops of both rocker supports so they are flush with the center support.

3. Trim the long straight side of the backrest at approximately the same angle as used to trim the rocker supports. This will allow the backrest to tilt slightly to the rear of the rocking horse when attached to the seat.

4. Position the head and backrest on the seat where indicated on the pattern. Use 2 screws to attach the backrest, and 3 screws to secure the head, as shown in Figure D. Remember to angle the screws into the backrest.

If you wish to add additional support, cut two extra 6-in.-long wooden support blocks, each ¾-in. by ¾-in., and fasten them on either side of the head with glue and small finishing nails.

5. Carefully center the top assembly (head, seat, and backrest) over the support assembly (2 rocker supports and the center support, as shown in Figure E. Fasten them together with glue and 4 nails driven through the top of the seat (2 nails into each of the rocker supports). You may use screws, but they must be countersunk to avoid scratching a child.

Recess the nails and fill in the nail holes with wood filler (optional).

6. To make sure the rockers are evenly attached to the rocker supports, we suggest you perform a temporary assembly:

a. Line the rockers up with the side edges of the 2 rocker supports and drill 2 small holes through each of the rockers. The holes will be more even if you tape the rockers together and drill through both at the same time.

b. Temporarily insert a nail through the hole drilled into the rocker and tap it into the side of the rocker support.

c. Place the assembled rocking horse on level ground and check the rocking action. If necessary, adjust the positioning on the rocker support so that the assembly rocks evenly.

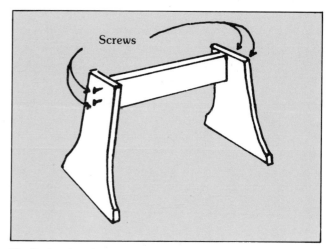

Fig. B. *Attach rocker supports to center support.*

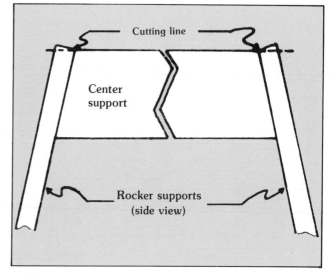

Fig. C. *Trim rocker supports flush with center support.*

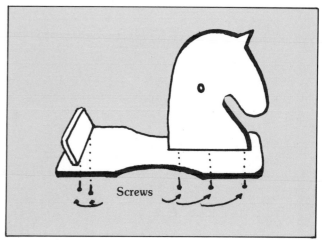

Fig. D. *Attach head and backrest.*

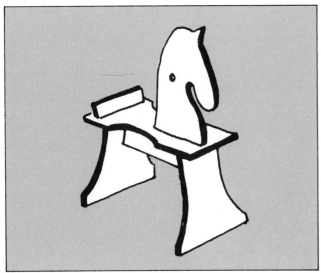

Fig. E. *Attach top assembly to support assembly.*

Fig. F. *Attach rockers and decorate.*

7. After you have determined that the rocking action is smooth and even, remove the nails and fasten the rockers to the rocker supports permanently with glue and screws.

8. Lastly, insert the ¾-in. wood dowel rod through the hole in the head and secure it with glue.

Decorating

You can either stain or paint the assembled rocking horse. Whatever you choose, make certain you use non-toxic materials to protect children. We painted our rocking horse bright yellow, and painted the mane brown, eyes blue (with black lashes), the bridle red, and completed the vine in green, the heart in red, and the flowers in red.

ABC BOOK

Materials

7 yds. of 36-in. wide canvas fabric. (If you can find it 60-in. wide, you need only 3½ yds.). Thinner fabric may be used, but it is best to line it so the letters don't show through.

Artist's acrylic paints (or fabric paint) in 5 basic colors (red, yellow, blue, black and white). With these 5 colors you can mix all the others.

For example:

    red + blue = purple
    red + yellow = orange
    blue + yellow = green
    red + blue + yellow = brown

    Add black to make a color darker.
    Add white to make a color lighter.

2 paint brushes — 1 fine and 1 medium width

Straight pins, white thread, scissors, yardstick, sewing machine, pencil and pinking shears

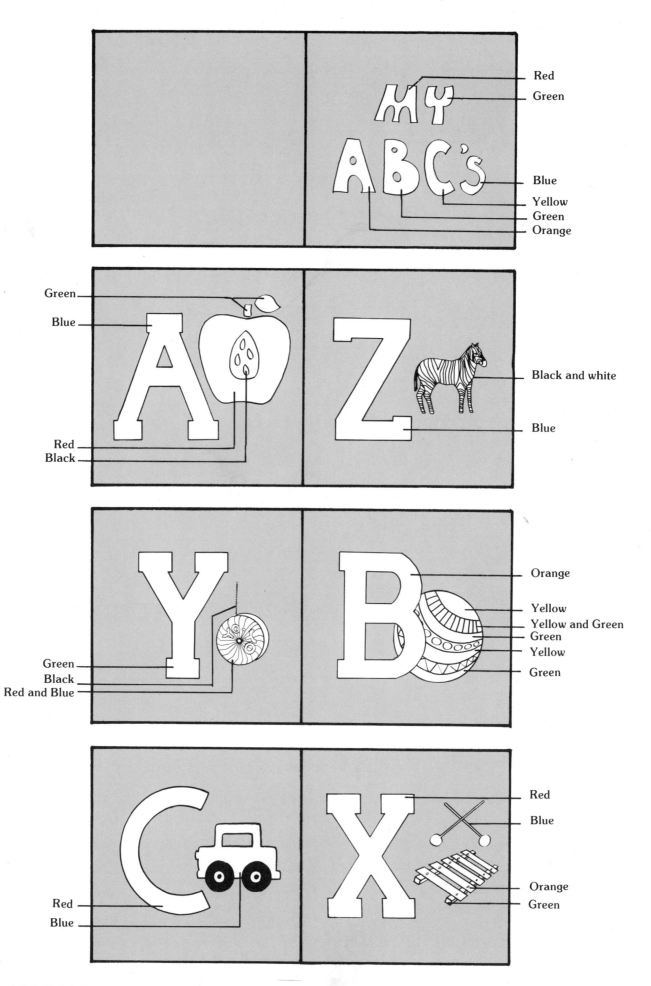

Cutting the fabric

You will need a large flat surface to work on, such as the kitchen table.

1. Press the canvas or other fabric to remove wrinkles.

2. Cut 14 canvas rectangles, each 15 × 28-in. These will be the pages of the ABC book. Rule each rectangle down the middle so you have 2 sides, each 15 × 14 in. Each side will be 1 page.

3. Follow the illustrations to place each letter on its appropriate page.

Painting

Acrylic paint as it comes from the jar or tube is usually a good thickness for fabric painting; however, because manufacturers vary, it is a good idea to practice and test a bit before beginning. Too thick paint will flake off later.

When you work with acrylics they dry fast, so work quickly. If the paint begins to dry while you are mixing or using it, add a drop of water and stir. Be careful not to add too much water, as thin paint may bleed into the fabric and blur the design. You can clean your brushes with water.

1. Follow the pattern and paint each of the designs. It is a good idea to begin at the top of the design and work down to avoid having to place your hands and brushes on already painted work.

2. A suggested color chart is provided for each of the designs. However, feel free to change any of the colors you wish.

3. When mixing a color, make sure you mix enough to complete the portion you are painting, as it is extremely difficult to remix and exactly match colors.

4. When you have finished painting, let the entire book dry overnight.

5. Place a cloth over each portion of the finished design and steam with a medium hot iron. This will set your design.

6. The book can then be washed gently in cold water or dry cleaned without color loss.

Finishing

1. Place the first 2 rectangles together back to back so that the "A" is on the reverse side of "My ABC's." Pin them together. Continue pinning the next 2 pages back to back, the next 2, and so on.

2. Stack the 7 resulting double-layered rectangles together. Check to make sure the pages are in the proper order—beginning with "A" and ending with "Z."

3. Sew each of the 7 pinned rectangles together on all 4 sides, and down the center page dividing line. Pink around all 4 edges.

4. Restack and pin the double rectangles and sew down the center of the stack to finish the book.

Fig. A. *Stitch around 4 sides; then stack the 7 doubled layers (3 layers shown).*

W
Blue
Red
Black
Green

D
Green
Yellow
Orange

E
Blue
Black outlines
Orange

V
Green
Red

I LOVE YOU

U
Yellow
Red
Blue

F
Orange
Yellow
Green

G
Green
Red
Blue

T
Orange
Red
Yellow
Green

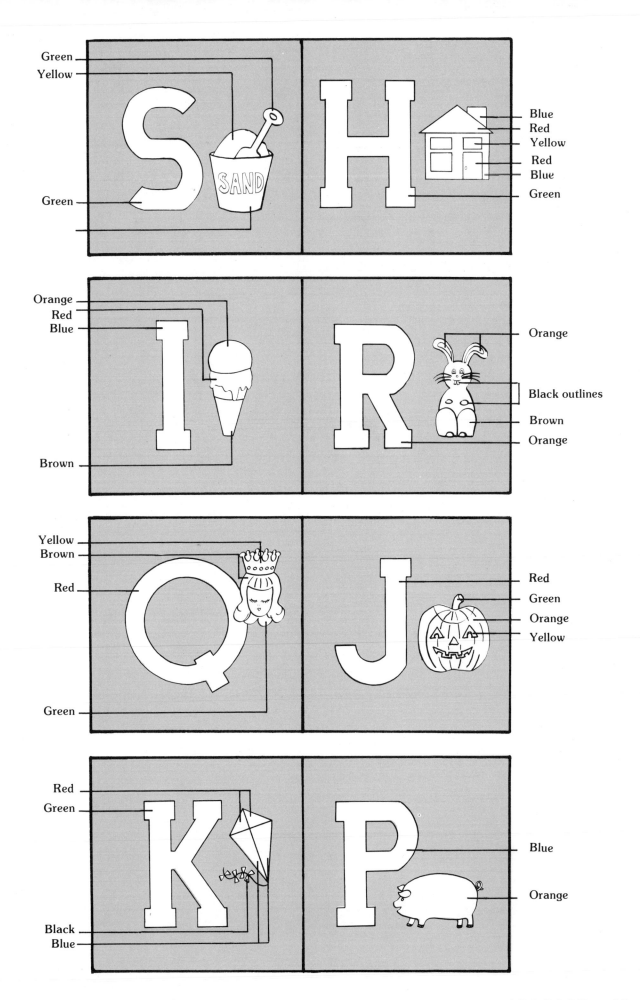

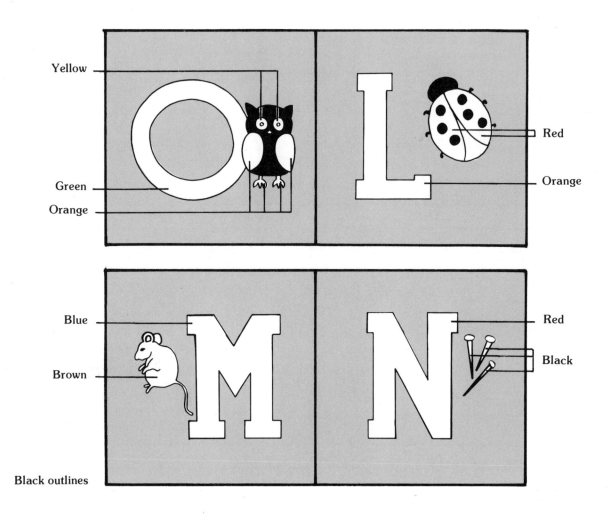

Yellow

Green

Orange

Red

Orange

Blue

Brown

Red

Black

Black outlines

Materials

To determine the materials necessary to build each plane, consult the materials chart.

In addition to the materials listed in the chart, you will need:

Sabre saw, jig saw, or hand coping saw.
Drill (electric is faster).
2 or 3 sheets each of medium and fine garnet sandpaper.
White glue or wood glue (aliphatic resin is best).

1-in. finishing nails.
Wood clamps or C-clamps to apply pressure to glued joints.
Rasp for shaping the body and nose cone of the biplane.
Hammer and scissors.
We purchased a propeller at a local hobby shop, but the propeller pattern for the triplane can be used for the biplane also.

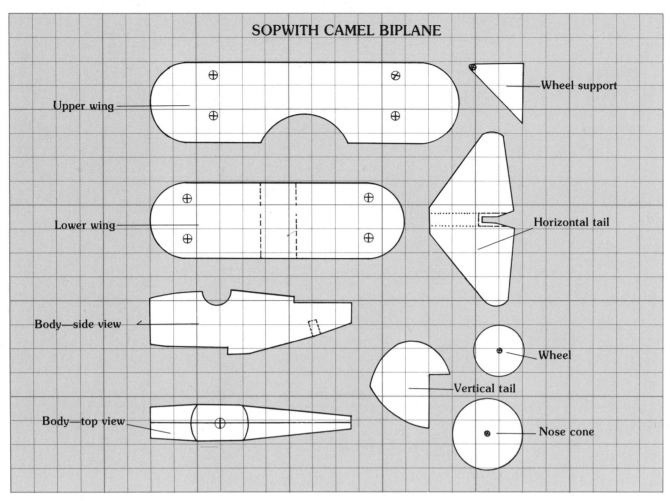

SOPWITH CAMEL BIPLANE

Upper wing

Wheel support

Lower wing

Horizontal tail

Body—side view

Wheel

Vertical tail

Body—top view

Nose cone

1 square = 1 inch

Biplane

Qty.	Pattern piece	Type of lumber*	Total length	Size drill bit	Other
1	Propeller stop	Slice of ½-in. diameter wood dowel	5-in.	¼-in. or ½-in.	3 metal washers with at least $9/16$-in. hole (or $5/16$-in. hole for ¼-in. dowel)
2	Wheels	½-in.	5-in.		
1	Wheel support	2 × 4	4-in.		"Pilot" requires 1-in. diameter wood drawer pull (or round finial or rubber ball) for head, and ½-in. wood dowel for neck (1½-in. long)
1	Axle	¼-in. dowel	5-in.		
1	Body	2 × 4	9-in.		
1	Skid	¼-in. dowel	3-in.		
1	Nosecone	2 × 4	4-in.		
1	Vertical tail	½-in.	4-in.		
1	Horizontal tail	½-in.	7½-in.		Small piece of felt for scarf
1	Upper wing	½-in.	14-in.		
1	Lower wing	½-in.	11-in.		
4	Wing supports	½-in. dowel 4½-in. long	18-in.		
1	Propeller support	¼-in. wood dowel	2½-in. long		

* ¼-in. or ½-in. plywood may be substituted for ½-in. lumber.

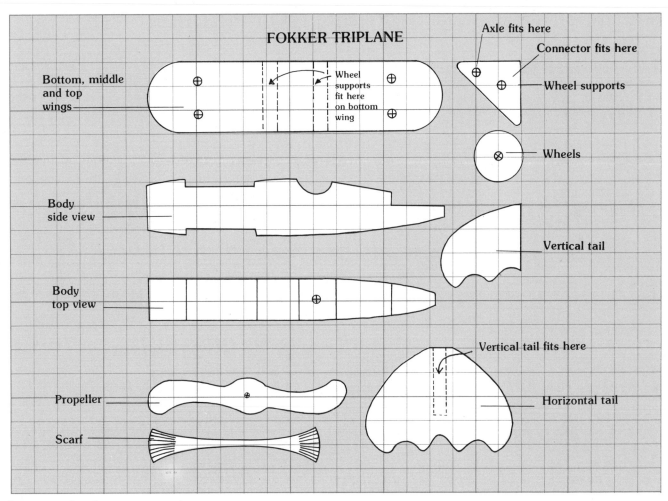

FOKKER TRIPLANE

Bottom, middle and top wings

Wheel supports fit here on bottom wing

Axle fits here

Connector fits here

Wheel supports

Wheels

Body side view

Vertical tail

Body top view

Vertical tail fits here

Propeller

Horizontal tail

Scarf

1 square = 1 inch

Triplane

Qty.	Pattern piece	Type of lumber*	Total length	Size drill bit	Other
2	Wheels	½-in.	5-in.	½-in.	Same additional materials as for biplane (above)
1	Wheel support connectors	½-in. diameter dowel	2½-in.		
1	Bottom wing	½-in.	13-in.		
1	Middle wing	½-in.	13-in.		
1	Top wing	½-in.	13-in.		
1	Propeller	½-in.	9-in.		
1	Body	2 × 4	14-in.		
1	Vertical tail	½-in.	4-in.		
1	Horizontal tail	½-in.	7-in.		
1	Propeller stop	Slice of 1-in. dowel	½ to 1-in. long		
4	Wing supports	½-in. dowel, 6-in. long	24-in.		
1	Skid	½-in. wood dowel	2-in.		
1	Axle	½-in. wood dowel	4-in. long		
1	Propeller support	¼-in. wood dowel	1-in.		

* ¼-in. or ½-in. plywood may be substituted for ½-in. lumber.

Cutting the pieces

1. Enlarge the scale pattern pieces. Directions for enlarging and transferring the full-size patterns to wood are given under "Toy Building Tips and Techniques" at the beginning of the book.

2. Cut the wood carefully along the outside lines of each pattern.

3. Cut the proper number and length of wooden dowel rods as listed on the chart.

Drilling and sanding

1. Drill all holes where indicated on the pattern pieces. Drill the same size hole as the diameter of the dowel rod which you are using. Drill a hole halfway through the center of the propeller stop to accommodate the dowel which supports the propeller.

2. Shape and size the biplane body with a wood rasp, following the pattern guidelines. Drill a hole into the center of the nose. This hole will later be used to attach the nose cone and propeller. Gently round and shape the biplane nose cone.

3. Thoroughly sand all pieces of wood. Begin with medium sandpaper and finish with fine. Sand until no sharp edges remain.

Assembly

1. Attach the wheel support to the lower wing first:

Biplane: Nail and glue the wheel support to the center of the lower wing.

Triplane: Wipe glue on the end of the wheel support connector dowel rod. Slide the wheel supports over each end of the connector dowel rod to form the wheel assembly.

Nail and glue the lower wing to the body of the plane.

2. Put the wing assembly together next. Wipe glue on the wing support dowel rods and insert through the drilled holes in the wings. Set aside to dry overnight.

3. Glue and nail the tail section together (vertical tail and horizontal tail) and let dry. Attach the tail section to the rear of the body.

4. For the biplane, wipe glue on the propeller support dowel and insert 1 end through the center of the nose cone and into the center hole which you drilled in the front of the body. For the triplane, simply insert the propeller support dowel rod into the hole in the front of the body.

5. Slip a washer over the extended portion of the dowel rod and slip the propeller onto the dowel. Wipe glue on the end of the dowel and attach the propeller stop.

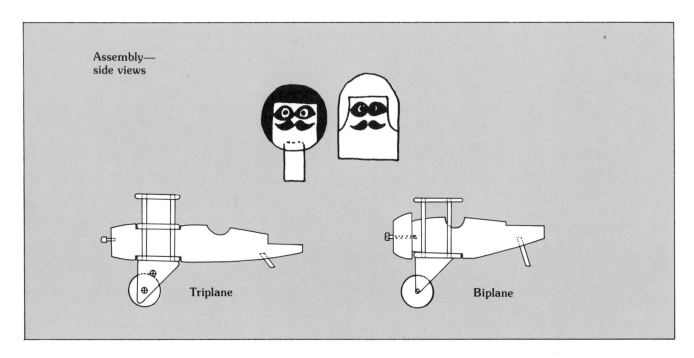

Assembly— side views

Triplane

Biplane

Adding the Wheels

1. Insert the axle dowel through the holes drilled in the wheel support.

2. Slip a washer onto each end of the axle dowel, and attach the wheels with a spot of glue.

3. Wipe glue on the end of the skid and attach it at the rear of the plane. Let the glue set overnight.

Finishing

We painted our biplane, and left the triplane the natural wood color. Children seem to like them either way, and they both look great. If you decide to paint, be sure you use non-toxic paint to protect little ones.

OLD-FASHIONED TRUCKS

These 3 trucks are fine examples of the early automobiles of the "good ole days." Generally chain-driven, these trucks became the workhorses of the twentieth century. They fulfilled a wide variety of jobs, from milk delivery to fire-fighting.

The trucks depicted here are 3 that kids love. They're easily built, with a minimum amount of expense.

Materials

Approximately 6 ft. of 1 × 6 clear pine
Small strip of 2 × 4 for hood
3 ft. of ⅜-in. dowel rod
2 ft. of 1¼-in. dowel rod (depending on the number of men you wish to make)

1¼-in. long finishing nails
Glue—white glue or Elmer's carpenter's glue is excellent

Tools

You'll need a hammer, sabre saw, and a drill.

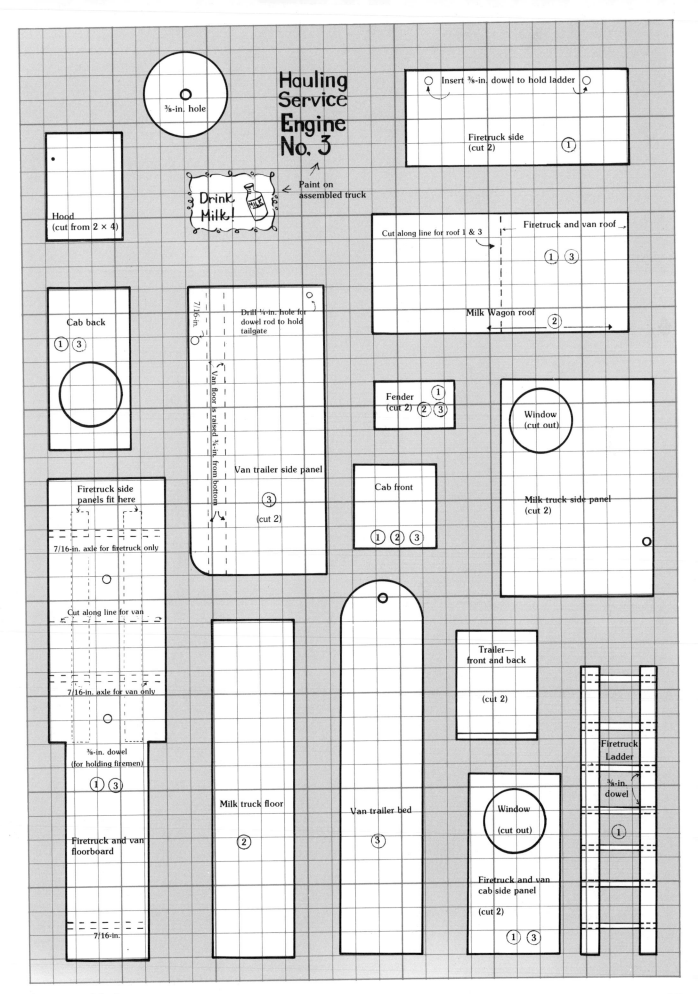

Hauling Service Engine No. 3

⅜-in. hole

Insert ⅜-in. dowel to hold ladder

Firetruck side
(cut 2)   ①

Hood
(cut from 2 × 4)

Drink Milk!   ← Paint on assembled truck

Cut along line for roof 1 & 3   Firetruck and van roof →
① ③

Milk Wagon roof   ②

Cab back
① ③

7/16-in.   Drill ¼-in. hole for dowel rod to hold tailgate

Van floor is raised ⅜-in. from bottom

Van trailer side panel

(cut 2)   ③

Fender   ①
(cut 2) ② ③

Window
(cut out)

Cab front

① ② ③

Milk truck side panel
(cut 2)

Firetruck side panels fit here

7/16-in. axle for firetruck only

Cut along line for van

7/16-in. axle for van only

⅜-in. dowel
(for holding firemen)

① ③

Firetruck and van floorboard

7/16-in.

Milk truck floor

②

Van trailer bed

③

Trailer—front and back

(cut 2)

Window
(cut out)

Firetruck and van cab side panel

(cut 2)

① ③

Firetruck Ladder

⅜-in. dowel

①

Construction

The frame and chassis for each of the toys are basically the same. The front hood and cab are identical for the fire engine and the hauling truck. The milk truck is the exception.

1. Cut out the pieces for the truck you are making according to the plans, following the numerical code on the plans.

2. Start with the chassis, cutting according to the truck that you are building (see plans). Use 1-in. pine for all pieces except the hood. Cut the hood from a 2 × 4.

3. Cut out the wheels from the 1-in. pine using a jig saw. Drill a ⅜-in. hole in the center of the wheel.

4. Drill the 2 holes ⁷/₁₆ to ½-in. in diameter for the axles. Drill these completely through the chassis.

5. Glue and nail the pieces together, starting with the hood and front fenders.

6. Put the cab together next—without the hood. Then nail the cab and hood onto the frame.

7. The truck trailer is put together as shown in the drawings. Nail all parts together and use glue. The trailer back is hinged by drilling a ¼-in. hole into the truck sides as shown and a ⁵/₁₆-in. hole into the tailgate so that it will swing easily. Hold the tailgate (back) in place with small nails temporarily, and drill the ¼-in. hole. Remove tailgate and expand hole in tailgate with ⁵/₁₆-in. bit.

8. The rear portion of the fire engine is positioned 1-in. from the edge of the frame so that the ladder will fit between the wheel and the side assembly.

9. Add the wheels using ⅜-in. dowel for the axle. Don't forget to use washers between the truck frame and the wheels so that the wheels will turn easily.

10. The ladder is made from strips of ¾-in. × ¾-in. wood. Nail them together with a small nail temporarily, and drill ⅜-in. holes as shown. Cut ⅜-in. dowels to length (as shown on drawings). Remove nail and glue the dowels in place.

11. You can paint the trucks any way you wish, or you can simply give them a coat of varnish and let the kids at them!

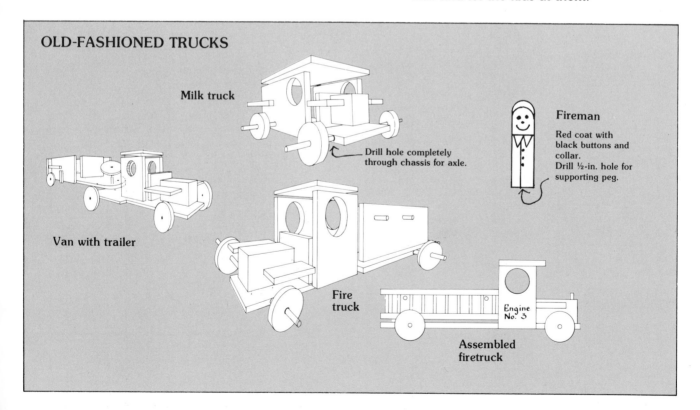

OLD-FASHIONED TRUCKS

Milk truck

Drill hole completely through chassis for axle.

Van with trailer

Fire truck

Assembled firetruck

Fireman

Red coat with black buttons and collar.
Drill ½-in. hole for supporting peg.

Engine No. 3

COLONIAL DOLLHOUSE

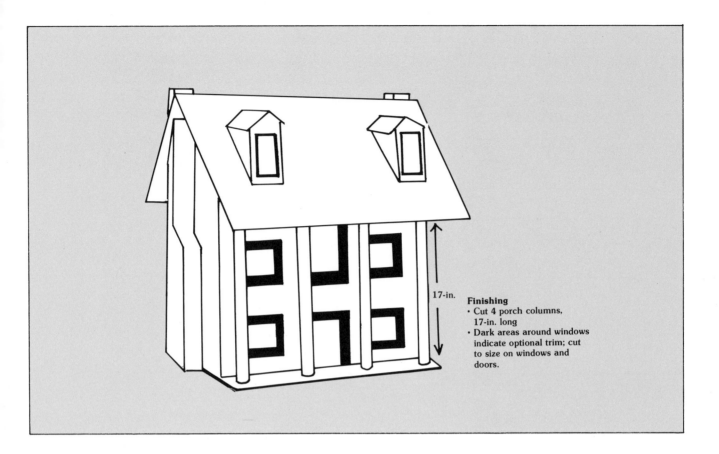

Finishing
- Cut 4 porch columns, 17-in. long
- Dark areas around windows indicate optional trim; cut to size on windows and doors.

Materials

Lumber	Quantity	Description
⅛-in. plywood	2 × 2 ft.	Gables
¼-in. plywood or particle board	4 × 8 ft.	Floors, ceiling, roof, walls, attic frame
1¼-in. diameter dowel rod	6 ft.	Porch columns
2 × 6 lumber	6 ft.	Chimneys
1-in. pine	scraps	Window frames

Miscellaneous

31-in. continuous hinge 1½-in. wide, or 3 to 4 small hinges; carpenter's wood glue, 1-in. nails.

Tools

Saw, hammer, drill, tape measure.

Assembly

Cut out pieces according to layout and sand each piece individually. Follow the assembly drawing. Glue and nail as shown. Assemble from bottom up.

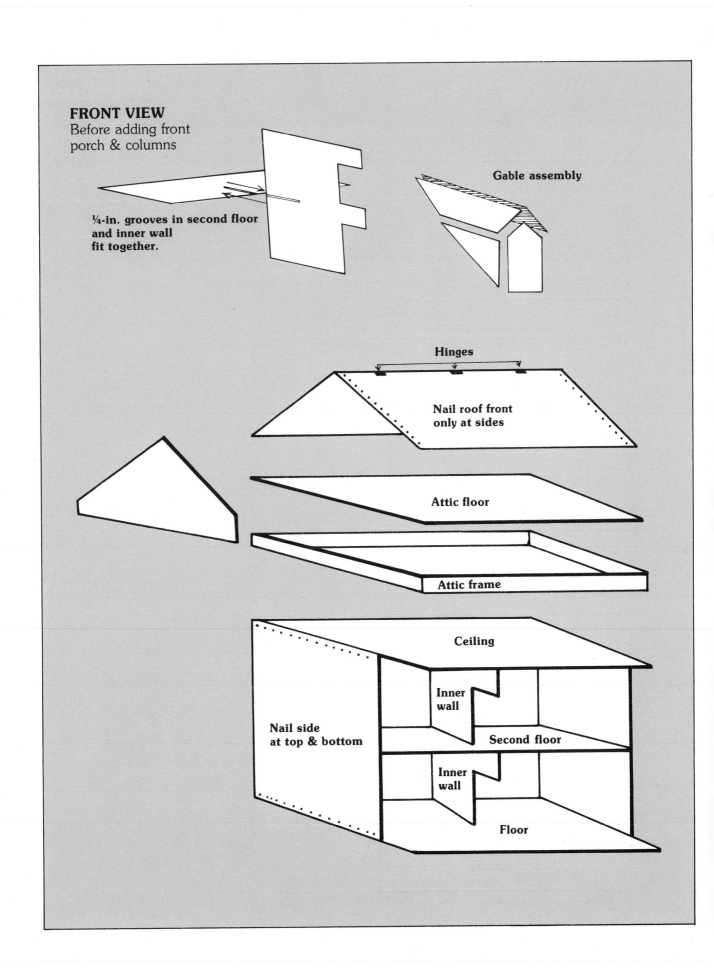

FRONT VIEW
Before adding front
porch & columns

¼-in. grooves in second floor
and inner wall
fit together.

Gable assembly

Hinges

Nail roof front
only at sides

Attic floor

Attic frame

Ceiling

Inner
wall

Nail side
at top & bottom

Second floor

Inner
wall

Floor

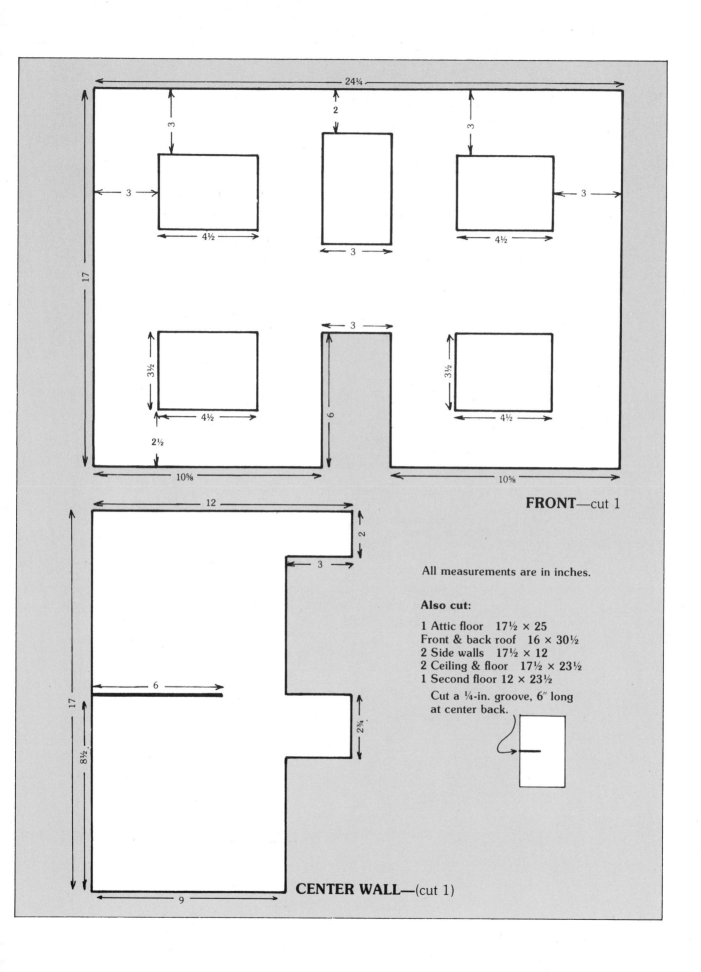

FRONT—cut 1

CENTER WALL—(cut 1)

All measurements are in inches.

Also cut:

1 Attic floor   17½ × 25
Front & back roof   16 × 30½
2 Side walls   17½ × 12
2 Ceiling & floor   17½ × 23½
1 Second floor 12 × 23½

Cut a ¼-in. groove, 6" long
at center back.

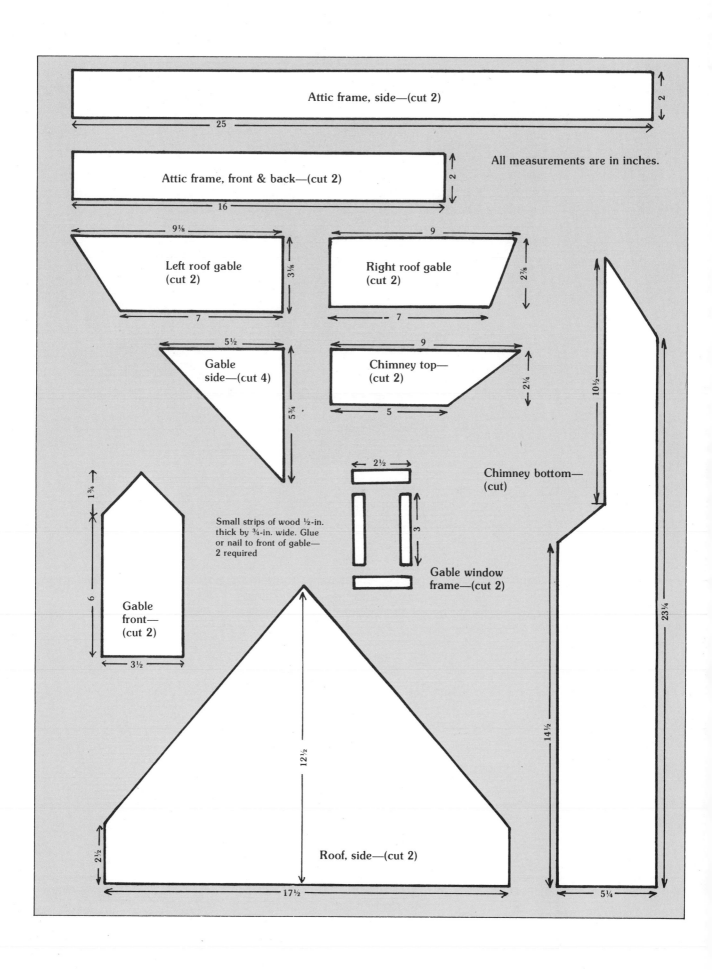

Attic frame, side—(cut 2)

25

2

Attic frame, front & back—(cut 2)

16

2

All measurements are in inches.

9⅛

Left roof gable
(cut 2)

3⅛

7

9

Right roof gable
(cut 2)

2⅞

7

5½

Gable
side—(cut 4)

5¾

9

Chimney top—
(cut 2)

2¼

5

Chimney bottom—
(cut)

10½

2½

3

Gable window
frame—(cut 2)

23¼

Small strips of wood ½-in.
thick by ¾-in. wide. Glue
or nail to front of gable—
2 required

1¾

6

Gable
front—
(cut 2)

3½

12½

Roof, side—(cut 2)

2½

17½

14½

5¼

COLONIAL DOLLHOUSE · 29

SUPER CAR

The Super Car is a great weekend project for a parent and child to work on together. While the finished project looks impressive, it is not complicated to build.

Materials

One 4 ft. by 8 ft. sheet of ¾-in. exterior grade plywood (for the car body)
12-in. by 18-in. piece of ½-in. exterior grade plywood for the windshield
2 × 8 pine lumber, 12 ft. long
2 × 4 clear pine 4 ft. long for front axle holder
8 ft. of 1 × 12 clear pine for fenders, front, and back of car
Two 1¼-in. diameter dowel rods for axles
One ⅝-in. diameter bolt, 6½-in. long, with nut and 2 washers
2 small pulleys
2 eyebolts
One box of 1½-in. long finishing nails
1 pine can of wood filler
Several short pieces of ¼-in. wooden dowel rod for axle pegs
Four 1½-in. wood screws (optional)
Soap, beeswax or other lubricant
Paint in the colors of your choice; non-toxic for children's safety

Tools

Sabre saw, hammer, nail set, 24-in. bar or pipe clamps, drill and drill bits, wood rasp, garnet sandpaper, and putty knife.

Materials for Super Car

Part No.	Description	Dimensions	Material	Qty.
1	Grille-top	1½-in. × 15-in. × ¾-in.	Pine	1
2	Grille-bottom	1½-in. × 13½-in. × ¾-in.	Pine	2
3-16	Head light & tail light	¾-in. × 3½-in. diam.	Pine	6
4	Hood ornament	4-in. long × 1¼-in. diam.	Dowel	1
5	Front	¾-in. × 12-in. × 7-in.	Pine	1
6	Hood	¾-in. × 12-in. × 12-in.	Plywood	1
7-30	Fender top front	¾-in. × 3¾-in. × 16-in.	Pine	1 ea.
8-31	Fender side front	¾-in. × 3¾-in. × 9-in.	Pine	1 ea.
12-33	Fender top rear	¾-in. × 3¾-in. × 12-in.	Pine	1 ea.
11-32	Fender side rear	¾-in. × 3¾-in. × 8½-in.	Pine	1 ea.
13	Fender support rear-top	¾-in. × 1½-in. × 9-in.	Pine	2
14	Fender support rear-side	¾-in. × 1½-in. × 8-in.	Pine	2
9	Fender support front-side	¾-in. × 1½-in. × 8-in.	Pine	2
10	Fender support front-top	¾-in. × 1½-in. × 13-in.	Pine	2
15	Body sides	¾-in. × 15½-in. × 37-in.	Plywood	1 ea.
17	Body back	¾-in. × 10¼-in. × 12-in.	Plywood	1
18	Body back contour	¾-in. × 3-in. × 12-in.	Plywood	1
19	Seat back	¾-in. × 12½-in. × 13½-in.	Plywood	1
20	Wedges	3-in. × 2-in. × 1½-in.	2 × 4	2
21	Seat bottom	¾-in. × 7-in. × 12-in.	Plywood	1
22	Dashboard	¾-in. × 9-in. × 12-in.	Plywood	1
23	Windshield	½-in. × 10-in. × 13½-in.	Plywood	1
24	Steering axle	1¼-in. diam. × 19-in.	Pine	1
25	Outside steering ring	¾-in. × 8-in. diam. w/6-in. diam. hole	Plywood	1
26	Inside steering ring	¾-in. × 3-in. diam. w/1¼-in. diam. hole	Plywood	1
27	Steering wheel	¾-in. × 8-in. diam.	Plywood	1
28	Front axle mounting platform	1½-in. × 7½-in. × 12-in.	2 × 8	1
29	Pivot block	1½-in. × 2½-in. × 4-in.	2 × 4	1
35	Front axle	1-in. diam. × 26-in. long	dowel	1
34	Front axle holder	1½-in. × 3½-in. × 17½-in.	2 × 4	2
36	Rear axle	1-in. diam. × 23-in. long	dowel	1
37	Outside wheel ring	¾-in. × 12-in. diam. with 8-in. hole	plywood	5
38	Inside wheel ring	¾-in. × 3-in. diam. w/1-in. diam. hole	plywood	5
39	Wheel	¾-in. × 12-in. diam.	plywood	5
40	Cotton rope	approximately ⅛-in. diam.		8 ft.
41	Pulley			
42	Eyebolt			
43	Dowel pins	⅝-in. × 6½-in.		
45	Washer			
46	Nut			

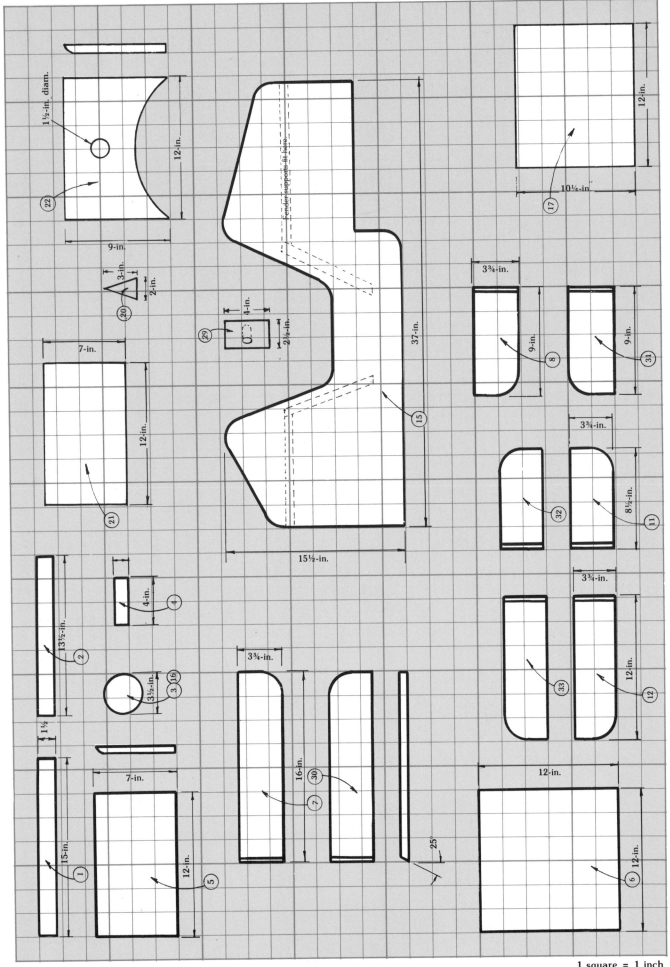

1½-in. diam.

22

12-in.

9-in.

20

3-in.

2-in.

29

4-in.

2½-in.

15½-in.

15

37-in.

Fender supports fit here.

17

10¼-in.

12-in.

7-in.

21

12-in.

3¾-in.

8

9-in.

31

9-in.

3¾-in.

32

8½-in.

11

2

13½-in.

4

4-in.

16

3

3½-in.

1½

33

12-in.

12

3¾-in.

1

15-in.

5

7-in.

12-in.

7

30

3¾-in.

16-in.

25

6

12-in.

12-in.

12-in.

1 square = 1 inch

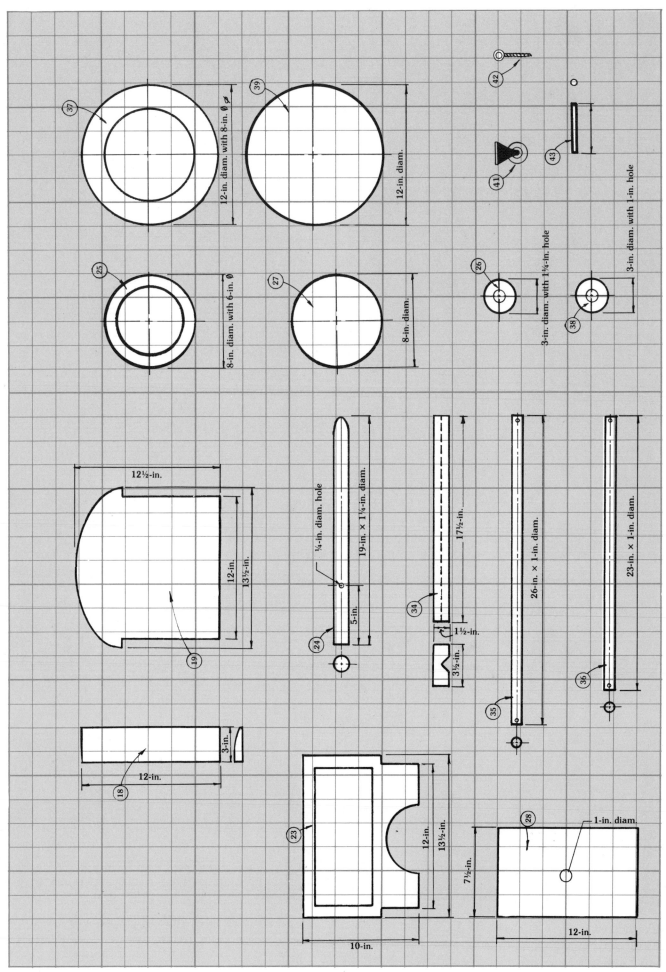

12-in. diam. with 8-in. ∅

12-in. diam.

8-in. diam. with 6-in. ∅

8-in. diam.

3-in. diam. with 1¼-in. hole

3-in. diam. with 1-in. hole

12½-in.

12-in.

13½-in.

¼-in. diam. hole

19-in. × 1¼-in. diam.

5-in.

17½-in.

1½-in.

3½-in.

26-in. × 1-in. diam.

23-in. × 1-in. diam.

3-in.

12-in.

12-in.

13½-in.

10-in.

7½-in.

1-in. diam.

12-in.

1 square = 1 inch

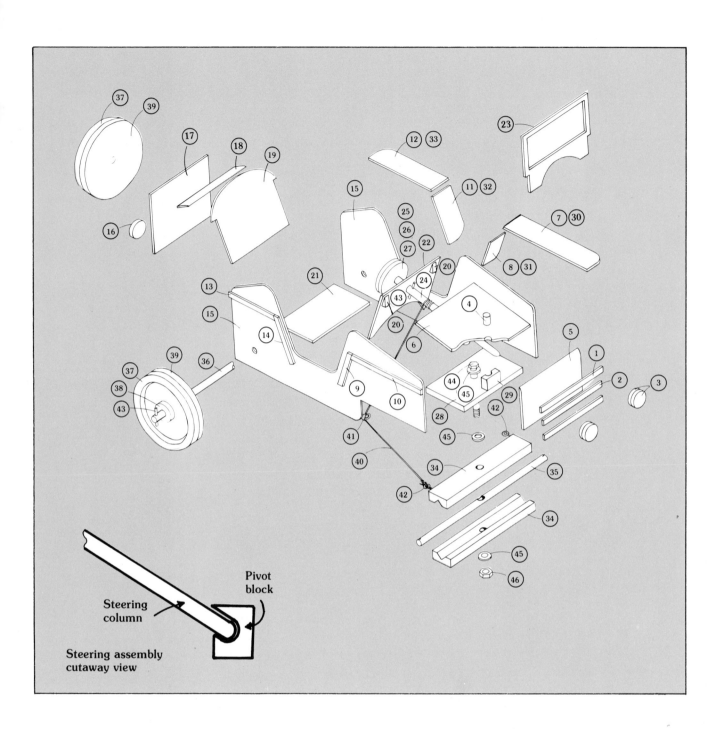

Steering
column

Pivot
block

Steering assembly
cutaway view

Assembly

1. To cut the 2 body pieces, we suggest that you first nail 2 pieces of plywood together temporarily. Then outline the car body sides and cut out both pieces at once with a sabre saw. Drill a 1-in. diameter hole for the rear axle before removing the holding nails.

2. Cut out all remaining pieces as specified on the list of materials. Make sure that you cut each piece from the correct materials. Drill all necessary holes.

3. Nail small 1-in. wood strips to each side of the car for fender supports. Glue and nails should be used for all assembly processes.

4. Position and glue the main car body parts. Hold them in place loosely with as few nails as possible (parts 17, 18, 19, 20, 21, 6, 22, 23, 28, and 5). Use bar or pipe clamps to pull the sides of the car together. Finish nailing in place. Recess all nails. Let the glue set up for 24 hours.

5. The front axle assembly is made from 2 × 4's with a V-groove cut down the length to accommodate a 1-in. axle as shown. Clamp and glue assembly together and allow to dry for 24 hours.

6. Place a small wood block (No. 29) as shown to hold the steering wheel column in place. Glue and nail in place (wood screws are preferable to nails). The block of wood should have a hole drilled to receive the slightly rounded tip of the steering column. The steering column is locked in place with a small ¼-in. dowel pin (No. 43). The pin should fit snugly against the back of the dash. Put some beeswax or other lubricant at the tip of the steering column to make the turning easier (see diagram).

7. Round off No. 5 and No. 17 with a rasp and sand flush with the sides and top of car.

8. Assemble all other parts following the exploded drawing.

9. Wheels should be glued and clamped for 24 hours. Then fill the open grain on the edge of the plywood with wood filler and sand smooth.

10. The steering assembly is a simple rope mechanism as shown. Drill a small hole in the center of the steering column and wrap 4 or 5 turns of rope through and around the column in opposite directions; pass through each pulley and attach the front axle as shown.

11. Paint car the colors of your choice.

12. Attach the wheels to the axles.

Note: This is intended as an indoor toy, and will not hold up if exposed to bad weather over a prolonged period of time.

CIRCUS TRAIN

Materials

5 ft. of 1 × 8 pine lumber
8 ft. of 2 × 4 pine lumber
8 ft. of 1 × 4 pine lumber
46 ft. of ⅜-in. diameter wooden dowel rod
Carpenter's wood glue
22 metal washers, with at least ⅜-in. diameter center hole
22 wooden wheels, each 2¼-in. in diameter, with ⅜-in. center hole
8 large-size cup hooks (or equivalent) to connect the finished train cars
A couple of sheets each of medium and fine garnet sandpaper

To paint the circus animals, you will need a small amount of paint in the following colors: red, black, white, and yellow. The other colors may be mixed with these 4. Be sure to buy non-toxic paint to protect little children. You also need a small paint brush.

Tools

Sabre saw, drill (electric is faster) with 2 drill bits: ⅜-in. and ½-in.

Cutting chart

Pattern piece	Qty.	Material description
Lion	1	1 × 8
Bear	1	1 × 8
Elephant	1	1 × 8
Monkey	1	1 × 8
Giraffe	1	1 × 8
Cage top	5	1 × 4**
Cage bottom	5	2 × 4
Cage bars	51	⅜-in. wooden dowel rods, 7¾-in. long
Axles	11	⅜-in. wooden dowel rods, 6-in. long
Wheels	22	¾-in. thick, 2¼-in. diameter wheels with ⅜-in. hole drilled in center
Engine body	1	2 × 4
Engine bottom floor	1	2 × 4
Engine roof	1	1 × 4

Cutting, drilling and sanding

1. Enlarge the graphed patterns to full size. Then consult the cutting chart to determine the quantity to be cut of each piece. Make sure you have chosen the correct width and thickness of wood for each piece. Use carbon paper and pencil to transfer the patterns to wood.

2. Following the cutting chart, cut the correct number and length of wooden dowel rods, and the correct number of wheels.

3. Drill holes in cage tops and bottoms and in the engine body and roof where indicated on the patterns. To make sure all holes are properly aligned, drill the holes in 1 cage top, then use that piece as a pattern to drill holes through the corresponding cage bottom. All of the holes drilled for cage bars should be ⅜-in. in diameter.

4. Drill ½-in.-diameter axle holes straight through the sides of the cage bottoms, as shown in Figure A. Exact placement is not necessary, as long as each train car looks the same.

5. Assemble cages as shown in Figure B. Wipe a little glue on the end of each cage bar, and insert it into the bottom of the cage. When all bars are glued in place on the cage bottom, fit the cage top over the bars so that it is level. Glue in place.

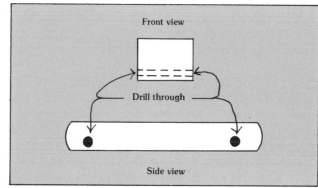

Fig. A. *Drilling axles.*

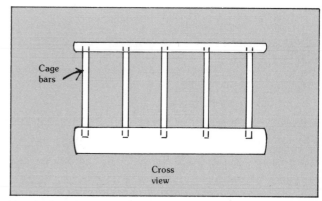

Fig. B. *Assemble cages.*

6. Drill ½-in.-diameter axle holes straight through the sides of the engine body. The engine has 2 axles in back and 1 axle in front. Be sure to leave enough space between the two back axles so that the wheels will not interfere with each other when rolling.

7. Cut the front of the engine bottom floor at an angle to form a cowcatcher as shown in Figure C.

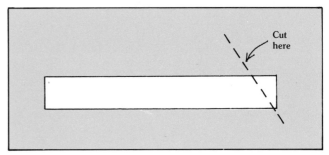

Fig. C. *Cut engine bottom floor.*

8. Drill a ⅜-in.-diameter hole in the top front of the engine to accommodate the engine ornament (a short piece of dowel rod). Cut the top of the engine body as shown in Figure D.

9. Glue a 1½-in. length of wooden dowel rod into the hole which you drilled in the top front of the engine as the engine ornament.

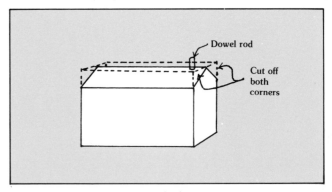

Fig. D. *Cut the top of the engine body.*

10. Wipe glue on the ends of each dowel rod used as cage bars on the engine, and insert each bar into the predrilled holes. Assemble the rest of the engine as shown in Figure E.

11. Allow the assembly for the engine and the cages to dry; then sand the roof tops to make sure that all cage bars are flush and smooth.

12. Paint each of the animals with bright, non-toxic paint. A suggested color guide is provided, but feel free to change any of the colors you wish. Let the paint dry overnight, then place the animals inside their cages. Screw cup hooks into the front and back of adjoining cars, and watch the smiles start when you hand it to your child!

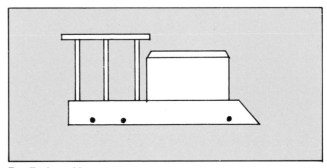

Fig. E. *Assemble engine.*

Color chart

Monkey— white face with brown eyes, nose, mouth. Brown body with white body outlines. Yellow banana with brown outlines.

Giraffe— orange body with black spots; black tail, eyes, horns and hooves.

Lion— orange body, face; yellow tail, mane, eyes, and area between mouth and nose. Outline in black.

Elephant— Gray body, white tusk, black toes, eye; outline ear in black.

Bear— Gold body outlined in black. White inner ears, eyes. Black eye pupils, nose. Red mouth.

The following 4 colors can be mixed. Amounts are approximate, since paint colors vary depending upon the manufacturer and the shade you choose.

Gold: ¾ yellow, ¼ black
Orange: ½ yellow, ½ red
Gray: ⅔ white, ⅓ black
Brown: ⅓ red, ⅓ yellow, ⅓ black

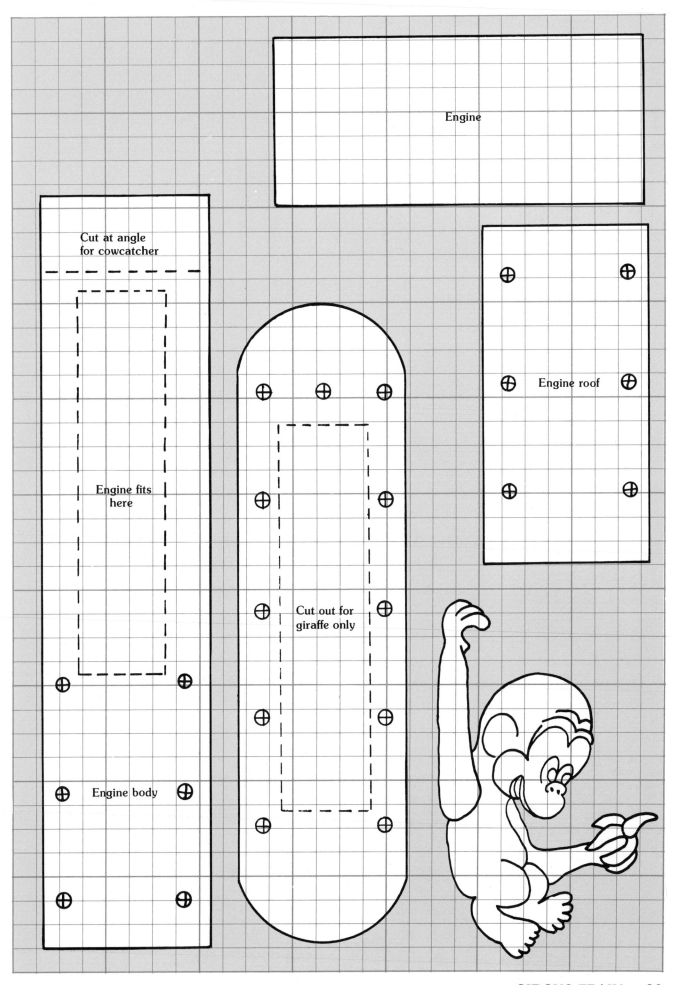

Engine

Cut at angle
for cowcatcher

Engine fits
here

Engine roof

Cut out for
giraffe only

Engine body

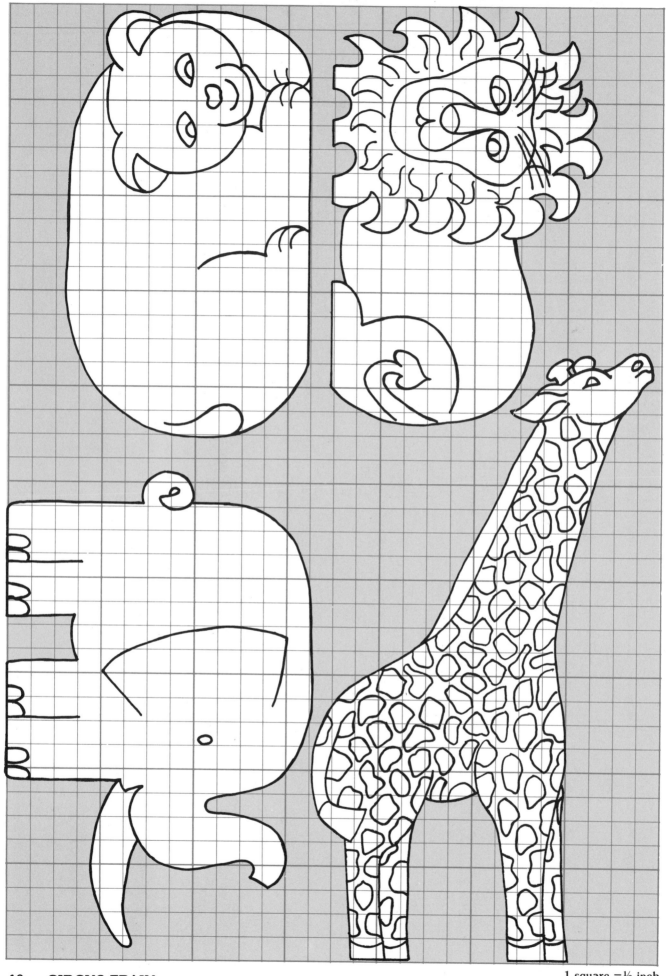

1 square = ½-inch

MINIATURE TOYS

Materials

1 -in. pine lumber scraps for car, plane, and train bodies
¼ -in. diameter wooden dowel rods for axles; ¾-in. dowel for the train engine and tank car
1 -in. diameter wooden wheels (you can substitute slices of a 1-in.-diameter wooden dowel rod)
8 small cuphooks for connecting the train cars
Sandpaper and wood glue

Tools

Coping saw, drill with three bits: ¼-in., ⁵/₁₆-in., and ½-in.

List of toys and pieces

Train:	Engine (nail ¾-in.-diameter dowel rod 2-in. long onto the front of the body as a boiler) Coal car Passenger car Tank car (nail ¾-in. dowel rod, 4½-in. long on top of the body as a tank) Caboose 20 wheels
Airplane:	Body, horizontal tail, vertical tail, propeller, wing Wood peg or short piece of dowel rod for propeller shaft. Small piece of wood for the propeller stop. 2 wheels
Limousine, pickup truck, sports car, and passenger car:	All have only 1 body piece, plus 4 wheels each.

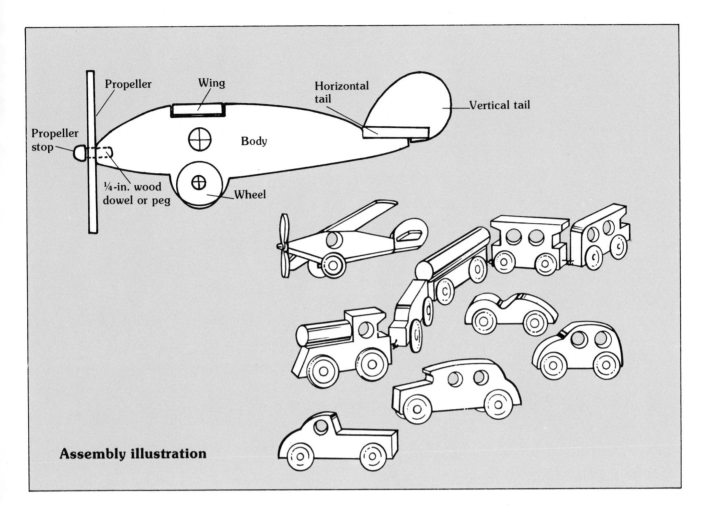

Assembly illustration

Cutting the pieces

1. Draw the individal pattern piece onto the wood. Consult the chart to determine the number of patterns required.

2. Cut carefully along the outside lines of each pattern.

3. Cut one 2-in. length of ¾-in. dowel rod, and one 4½-in. length of ¾-in. dowel rod.

Drilling and sanding

1. Drill ⁵⁄₁₆-in. holes through the toy body for axles where indicated.

2. Drill all window holes with a ½-in. drill bit where indicated.

3. Thoroughly sand all pieces to remove splinters and sharp edges.

Assembly

Each toy (with the exception of the airplane) has only 1 body piece. To assemble the airplane, follow the assembly diagram shown.

1. Cut axles (¼-in. dowels) to length, and insert through axle holes in the toy body. Attach wheels with a spot of glue and let dry for several hours.

2. To connect the train cars, screw a small cup hook into the back and front of adjoining cars. Pinch the cup hooks together if you wish the train to remain assembled.

3. Nail the 4½-in.-long ¾-in. dowel rod to the top of the tank car. Nail the 2-in. length of dowel rod to the front of the train engine.

We painted our toys with bright non-toxic paint, but you can also leave them the natural wood color or stain them.

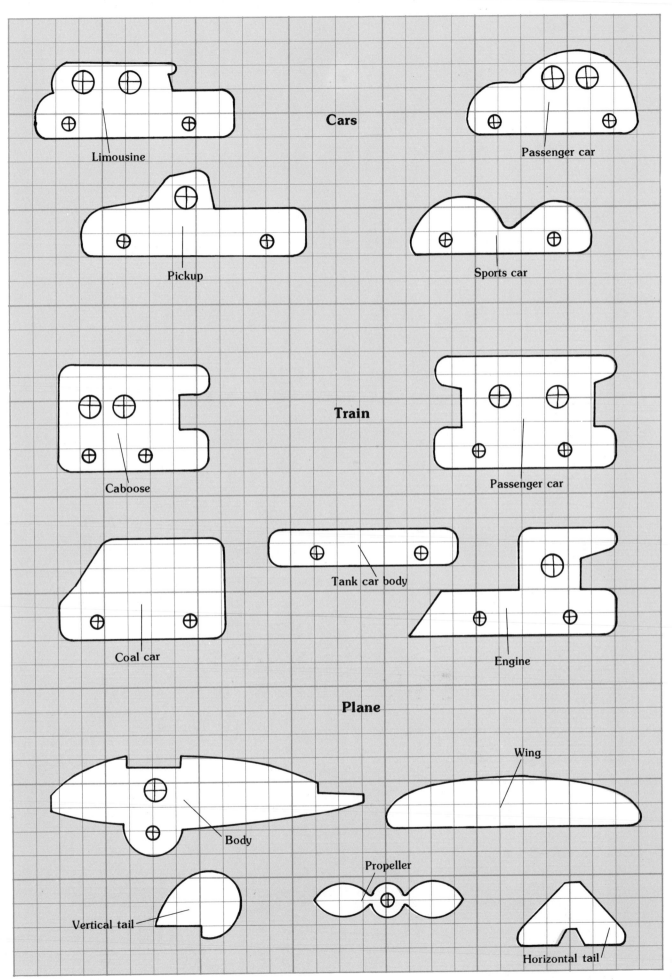

Cars

Limousine

Passenger car

Pickup

Sports car

Train

Caboose

Passenger car

Coal car

Tank car body

Engine

Plane

Wing

Body

Propeller

Vertical tail

Horizontal tail

MATILDA DOLL AND CRADLE

Materials

Small amounts of scrap fabric for pattern pieces:

       White (or flesh-colored)—body, leg, arm

       Small calico print—sleeve, dress top, skirt

       Contrasting solid—apron top, skirt front, strap, sash tie end, sash front

       Dark calico print or solid—shoes

       Light solid—pantalettes

       Fiberfill for stuffing doll body

Notions: Embroidery thread—blue, brown and pink

           ¼-in. wide elastic (for pantalette waist)

           Brown yarn for hair and large needle for yarn

           Trim lace (optional)

           1 small snap

           Straight pins, needle, thread to match fabrics, scissors

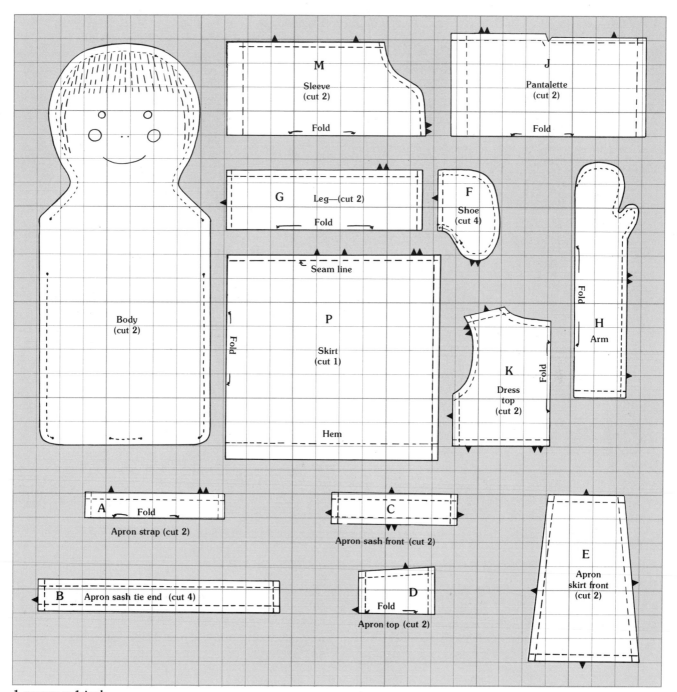

M
Sleeve
(cut 2)
Fold

J
Pantalette
(cut 2)
Fold

G Leg—(cut 2)
Fold

F
Shoe
(cut 4)

Body
(cut 2)

Seam line

P

Skirt
(cut 1)

Fold

Hem

K

Dress
top
(cut 2)

Fold

H
Arm

Fold

A Fold
Apron strap (cut 2)

C
Apron sash front (cut 2)

B Apron sash tie end (cut 4)

D
Fold
Apron top (cut 2)

E
Apron
skirt front
(cut 2)

1 square = 1 inch

Cutting the pattern pieces

Enlarge the pattern pieces onto tracing paper or newspaper. Use the resulting full-size pattern as you would any other fabric pattern, pinning it to the fabric and cutting it out.

When cutting patterns, pay particular attention to "Place on Fold" notations, and be sure to cut the number of pattern pieces specified.

Sewing

Body

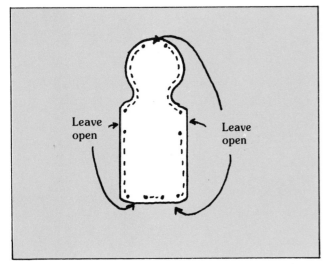

Fig. A. *Body.*

1. Place right sides together. Sew along seam allowance, leaving openings for legs, arms, and between ●'s at the top of the head.

2. Clip curves, turn right side out and press, turning the seam allowances to the inside.

3. Stuff with fiberfill.

Shoes and legs

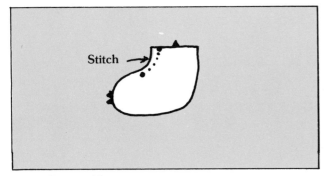

Fig. B. *Shoes and legs.*

1. Sew 2 shoe pieces (F), right sides together between ●'s.

2. Matching ▲'s, sew leg bottom to shoe tops, with shoe seam in the center of leg.

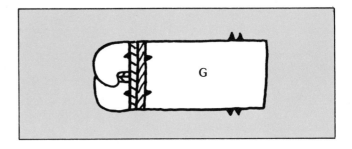

3. Fold leg right sides together and sew down the back of leg and around the shoe. Leave top of leg open.

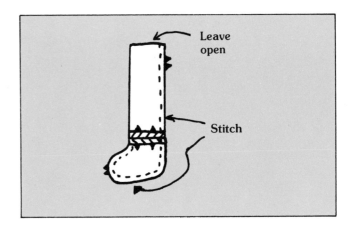

4. Clip curves, turn right side out and press.

5. Stuff leg and shoe with fiberfill.

Arms

1. Sew arm (H) right sides together along side seam and hand.

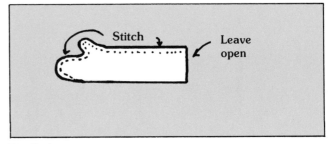

Fig. C. *Arm.*

2. Clip curves, turn right side out and press.

3. Stuff with fiberfill.

Finishing body

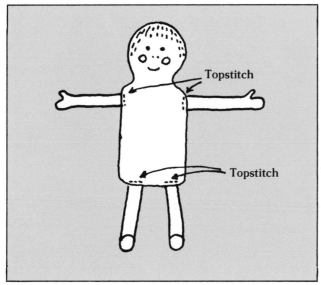

Fig. D. *Body.*

1. Pin arms (thumbs up) in arm openings on body. Topstitch in place.

2. Press top of leg so toe points to front and seam is at center back.

3. Pin legs (toes to front) in leg openings on body. Topstitch in place.

4. Whipstitch top of head together.

5. Embroider eyes (blue), nose (black), cheeks and mouth (pink). Use satin stitch to embroider.

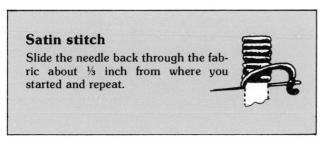

Satin stitch
Slide the needle back through the fabric about ⅓ inch from where you started and repeat.

Fig. E. *Satin stitch.*

6. Attach hair along dashes and on back of head. Thread needle, pull through fabric, and tie. For long hair, leave both tie ends long. Cut for short hair.

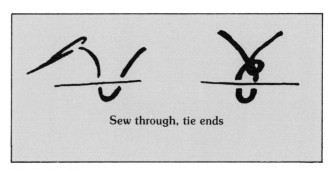

Sew through, tie ends

Fig. F. *Attach hair.*

7. We tied the hair in ponytails on both sides of the head.

Pantalettes

1. Place pantalette pieces right sides together. Sew center front and back seams.

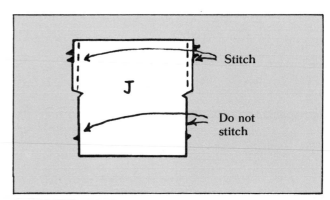

Stitch

J

Do not stitch

Fig. G. *Stitch pantalettes.*

2. Refold stitched pantalettes so center front and center back seams match, and sew center leg seams.

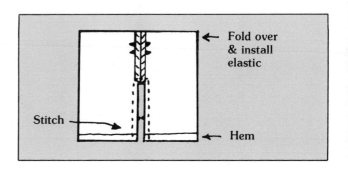

Fold over & install elastic

Stitch

Hem

3. Hem bottom of pantalette legs; install elastic at the waist. Add lace to the bottom hem if desired.

Dress

1. Place dress tops (K) right sides together and sew shoulder seams. Slit the center back and hem raw edges.

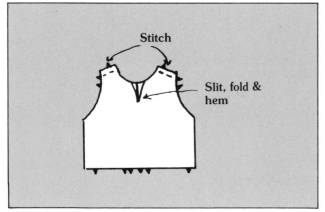

Fig. H. *Sew dress tops.*

2. Turn the raw edges to the inside around the neck and topstitch. Add lace to the neck if desired.

3. Sew snap at neckline in back.

4. Gather top sleeve (M) and sew to open armhole right sides together. Ease to fit.

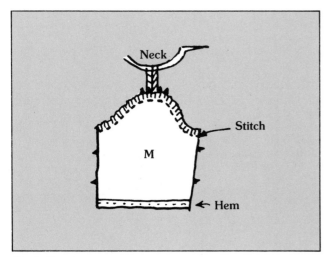

Fig. I. *Sew sleeves.*

5. Hem bottom of sleeve; add lace if desired.

6. Sew underarm and side seams.

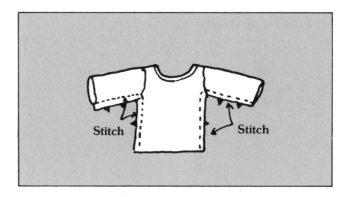

7. Turn up hem allowance on skirt (P) and stitch. Add lace if desired.

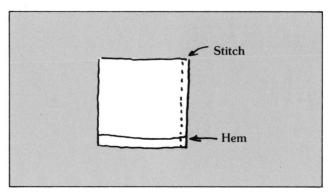

Fig. J. *Stitch and hem.*

8. Gather skirt along top gathering line, leaving seam area ungathered.

9. Sew skirt center back seam with right sides together.

10. Matching ▲'s, sew skirt to dress top (right sides together), easing gathers to fit.

Apron

1. Fold apron straps (A) right sides together. Sew along 3 sides, leaving 1 end open. Turn and press. Set aside.

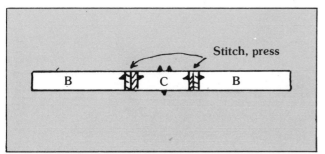

Fig. K. *Stitch and press apron straps.*

2. Sew apron sash tie ends (B) to apron sash front (C). Press seams open.

3. Matching ▲'s (right sides together), sew apron top (D) and apron skirt (E) to center of apron sash front. Clip at all 4 corners and press.

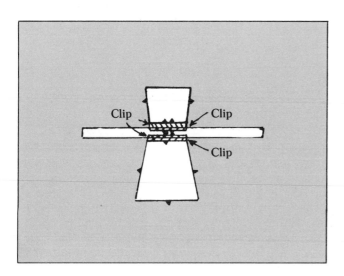

4. Repeat steps 1 through 3 for other apron pieces B, C, D, and E.

5. Pin 2 assembled apron sides right sides together, and sew around all edges, leaving apron top open. Clip corners and turn right side out. Press the top seam allowance to the inside.

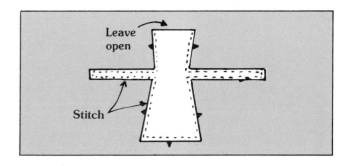

6. Pin the open end of apron straps (A) at either side of open apron top as shown. Topstitch across apron top to hold straps.

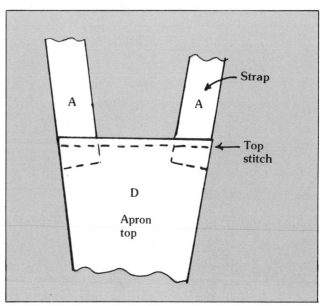

Fig. L. *Finish apron.*

7. Dress doll, tack apron straps in place at back and tie the apron in a bow in back.

DOLL CRADLE

Materials

4 × 4 ft. sheet of solid core plywood (or equivalent), ½-in. thick
Handful of finishing nails ¾-in. long
Wood glue, 4 sheets of sandpaper; 2 medium and 2 fine
Wood filler (optional) to cover nail holes
Masking tape

Tools

Ruler, hammer, sabre saw (or coping saw), nailset, to recess nails (a large nail will substitute).

Cutting and sanding

Cut the following pieces from ½-in. plywood:

Quantity	Code	Description
1	A	Back
1	B	Front
2	C	Side
1	D	Canopy front
2	E	Canopy side
1	F	Canopy top
2	G	Rocker
1	H	Bottom
4	J	Rocker support

Enlarge each pattern piece onto tracing paper or newspaper. Tape the pattern onto the plywood and trace around it. To cut 2 identical pieces, cut the first piece and use it as a pattern to cut the second.

It is easier to sand each piece just prior to final assembly. Begin with medium sandpaper and finish with fine.

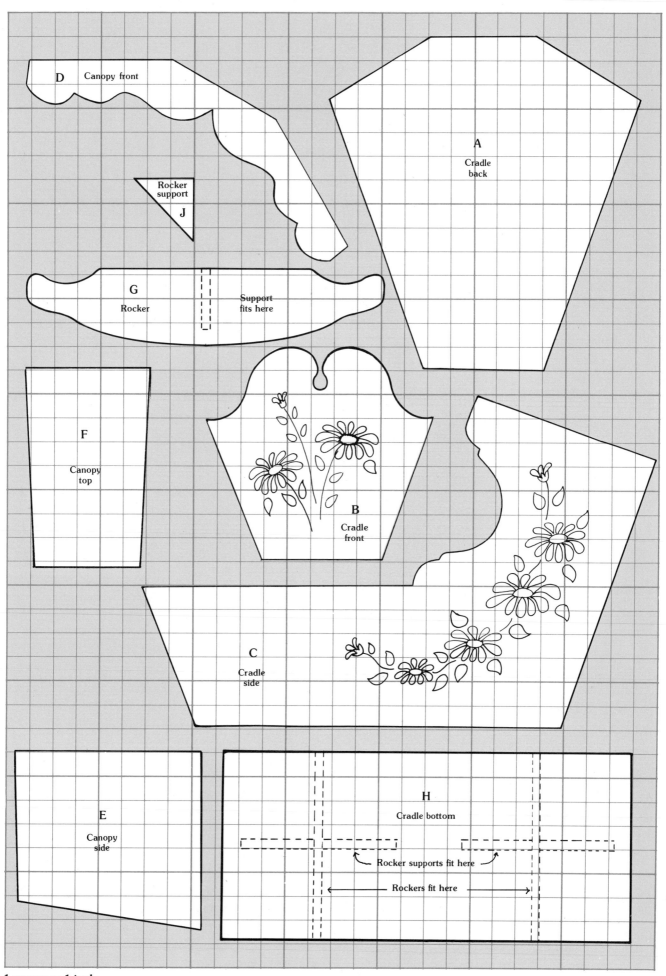

D Canopy front

Rocker
support
J

A
Cradle
back

G
Rocker

Support
fits here

F
Canopy
top

B
Cradle
front

C
Cradle
side

E
Canopy
side

H
Cradle bottom

← Rocker supports fit here →

← Rockers fit here →

1 square = 1 inch

CRADLE · 51

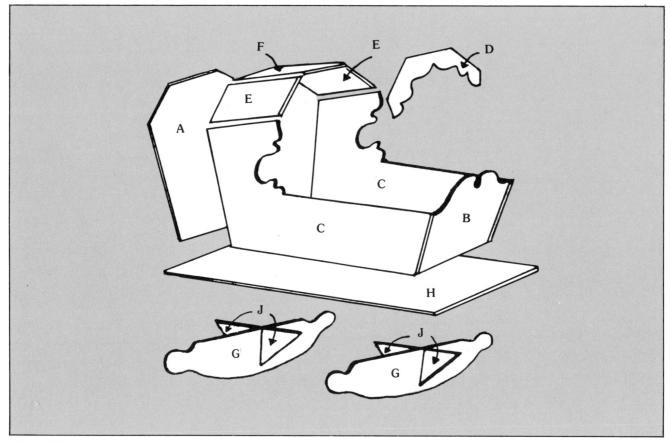

Fig. M. *Assemble cradle.*

Assembly

Use a temporary assembly method (specified below) on both the top of the cradle and bottom portion of the cradle. After the correct fit has been determined for both the top and bottom assemblies, nail and glue them; then join the two assemblies.

Top

1. Nail cradle back (A) and front (B) between sides (C).

2. Fit canopy front (D) between the top wings of cradle sides (C).

3. Add canopy sides (E) so that they cover the raw edges of canopy front (D) and cradle back (A).

4. Trim the long edges of canopy top (F) at a slight angle to fit flush with the 2 canopy side pieces (E).

Bottom

1. Make a temporary assembly, attaching rockers (G) to cradle bottom (H). Check the rocking action. When the rocking action is even, nail and glue the rockers in place. Nail through the cradle bottom and into the rockers.

2. Add 2 rocker supports (J) to each rocker; 1 on either side.

Finishing

1. Attach the top assembly to the bottom with glue and nails. Nail through the cradle bottom and into the raw edges of the assembled top.

2. Designs have been provided to decorate the front and side of the finished cradle. We painted the leaves and vines green, the flower petals white, and the flower centers yellow. The rest of the cradle may be stained over the design painting, or painted the color of your choice.

TRUCKS AND VANS

Materials and tools

Consult the chart to determine the materials necessary to build each vehicle. In addition to the materials listed in the chart, you will need a sabre saw, a drill, 2 or 3 sheets each of medium and fine sandpaper, wood glue, and a wood clamp or 2 C-clamps. An optional help is a circle-cutting attachment for a ¼-in. electric drill.

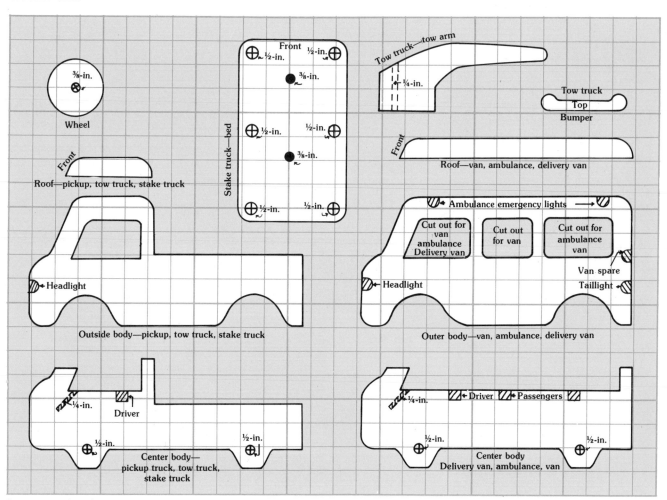

1 square = 1 inch

List of parts for trucks and vans

	Qty.	Pattern piece	Type of lumber	Total length	Drill bits	Other
Ambulance	1	Center body	2 × 6	12-in.	½-in.	1 Driver
	2	Outer body	1 × 6	24-in.	⅜-in.	4 metal washers with
	1	Roof	2 × 6	12-in.		at least ½-in.
	2	Axles	⅜-in. dowel	8-in.		diameter hole
	4	Wheels	1-in. lumber	12-in.		steering wheel &
	4	Head & Taillights	½-in. dowel*	3-in.		column
	4	Roof lights	1-in. dowel	5-in.		
			⅜-in. dowel	4-in.		
Van	1	Center body	2 × 6	12-in.	½-in.	Same as above
	2	Outer body	1-in. lumber	24-in.	⅜-in.	plus 2 additional
	1	Roof	2 × 6	12-in.		"passengers"
	2	Axles	⅜-in. dowel	8-in.		
	5	Wheels	1-in. lumber	15-in.		
	4	Head & Taillights	½-in. dowel*	3-in.		
	1	Spare tire holder	⅜-in. dowel	2-in.		
Delivery van	1	Center body	2 × 6	12-in.	½-in.	Same as above
	2	Outer body	1 × 6	24-in.	⅜-in.	
	1	Roof	2 × 6	12-in.		
	2	Axles	⅜-in. dowel	8-in.		
	4	Wheels	1-in. lumber	12-in.		
	4	Head & Taillights	½-in. dowel*	3-in.		
Pickup truck	1	Center body	2 × 6	12-in.	½-in.	Same as above
	2	Outer body	1 × 6	24-in.	⅜-in.	plus
	1	Roof	2 × 6	4-in.		2 bed pins (⅜-in.
	2	Axles	⅜-in. dowel	8-in.		dowel, a total of 3-
	4	Wheels	1-in. lumber	12-in.		in.)
	2	Headlights	½-in. dowel*	1½-in.		
	1	Bed	1 × 6	8-in.		
	6	Stakes	½-in. dowel	20-in.		
Tow truck	1	Center body	2 × 6	12-in.	½-in.	Same as above
	2	Outer body	1 × 6	24-in.	⅜-in.	plus
	1	Roof	2 × 6	4-in.		⅜-in. dowel 3-in.
	1	Tow arm	2 × 6	8-in.		long
	2	Axles	⅜-in. dowel	8-in.		
	4	Wheels	1-in. lumber	12-in.		
	2	Headlights	½-in. dowel*	1½-in.		
	1	Bumper	1-in. lumber			
	1	Roof light	1-in. dowel	1-in.		
			⅜-in. dowel	1-in.		

* Wood plugs may be substituted

Cutting the pieces

1. Enlarge and transfer each pattern piece to the correct thickness and width of wood (1 × 6, 2 × 4, etc.) as indicated on the chart. To make 2 pieces exactly alike, tape 2 thicknesses of wood together with masking tape, draw the pattern onto the top piece of wood, and cut them both out at the same time. Or cut 1 and use it as a pattern to cut the second piece.

2. Cut the wood carefully along the outside lines of each pattern.

3. Cut the proper number of wheels (listed on the chart). Cut two 4-in. lengths of ⅜-in.-diameter wooden dowel rod for each vehicle, which will be the axles.

Drilling and sanding

1. Drill all holes ⅜-in. deep unless otherwise indicated. Drill two ½-in. holes through each vehicle body for the axles where indicated on the pattern. Drill as straight as possible so the wheels will be even on the finished toy.

2. Drill ½-in. holes for "people" and ¼-in. holes for the steering wheel column, as indicated on the center body pattern.

3. Drill ⅜-in. holes through the exact center of all wheels.

4. Thoroughly sand all cut pieces of wood. Begin with medium sandpaper and finish with fine. Sand until no sharp edges remain.

Assembly

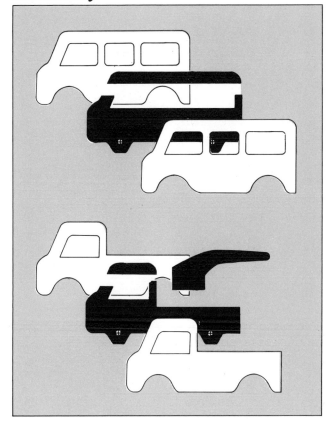

Fig. A. *Assemble vehicles.*

Each vehicle has 4 main body pieces: 1 middle piece of 2-in.-thick lumber, 2 outside pieces and the roof of 1-in.-thick lumber.

1. Wipe a thin coat of glue on each of the 1-in.-thick outer pieces on the side which faces the middle of the vehicle.

2. Place the glued pieces on each side of the middle body and press in place tightly with your hands.

3. Tightly clamp the assembled vehicle (or place a heavy weight on top) and allow the glue to dry overnight.

Adding the wheels

1. Insert the 4-in. lengths of wood dowel through the axle holes.

2. Slip a washer onto both ends of each axle dowel.

3. Attach the proper size wheels with a spot of glue. Let the glue set overnight.

Details

Headlights and taillights—

Use wood plugs, or follow these instructions:

a. Drill ⅝-in. holes into the front and back of the vehicle.

b. Cut ½-in.-long pieces of ⅝-in. dowel for each light.

c. Insert the dowel into the holes with a dab of glue.

Tow truck roof light—

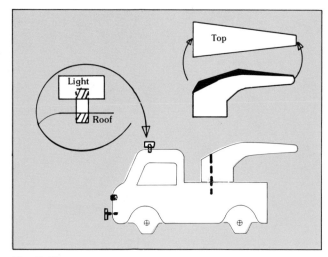

Fig. B. *Tow car.*

a. Assemble the roof light as shown in the diagram.

b. Drill a ⅜-in. hole into the cab roof and insert the light.

Tow arm—

a. Shape the arm as shown in the diagram.

b. With the tow arm in place, drill a ⅜-in. hole through the center of the arm and into the center of the body as shown in the diagram.

c. Insert and glue a 1¾-in.-long (⅜-in. diameter) dowel into the hole.

Bumper—

a. Drill ⅜-in. holes into the front of the truck below each headlight, and corresponding holes through the bumper.

b. Attach the bumper to the truck with two 1-in.-long pieces of ⅜-in. dowel.

Stake truck bed and stakes—

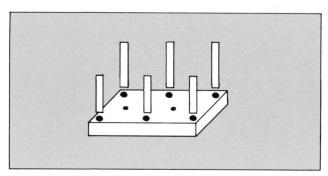

Fig. C. *Stake car bed.*

a. Drill ⅜-in. holes (1¼-in. deep) through the bed into the body. Drill ½-in. holes into the bed for stakes, as indicated on the pattern.

b. Insert two 1¼-in. lengths of dowel rods (⅜-in. in diameter) into the center holes to connect the bed to the body.

c. Glue six ½-in. dowels (3-in. long) into the bed as stakes.

Ambulance emergency roof lights—

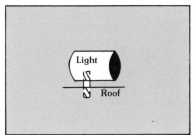

Fig. D. *Ambulance emergency light.*

a. Drill four ⅜-in. holes in the roof where indicated on the pattern.

b. Cut four ⅜-in. dowels, each 1-in. long.

c. Cut four 1-in. dowels, each 1¼-in. long.

d. Assemble and glue in place as shown in the diagram.

Van spare tire—

a. Drill a ⅜-in. hole into the back of the body. Wipe glue on a ⅜-in. dowel (1¼-in. long) and insert it into the hole.

b. Glue the spare tire onto the dowel.

Finishing

You can leave your toys natural wood, or paint them with non-toxic paint. Several suggested designs are shown.

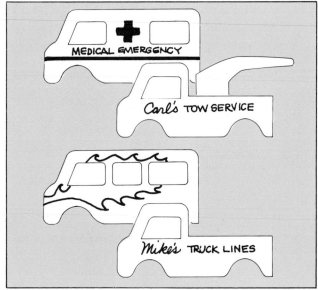

Fig. E. *Designs.*

Adding the little "person" (optional)

To add the driver to your vehicle, drill a ½-in.-diameter hole into the center body piece where the driver or passengers would "sit." Wipe glue on the end of the wood dowel rod, and insert it in the hole. Allow it to dry overnight.

Fig. F. *"Person"*

Adding the steering wheel

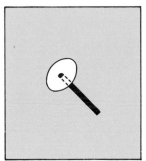

Fig. G. *Steering wheel.*

1. Wipe glue on both ends of a 2-in.-long (¼-in.-diameter dowel rod.

2. Insert 1 end through the center of a 1-in. wheel and the other end into the hole drilled into the center body.

19TH CENTURY TRAIN

Materials and tools

To determine the correct size lumber for each piece of each train car, consult the materials chart. In addition to the materials listed on the chart, you will need: a sabre saw (or hand coping saw), scissors, a drill, several sheets each of medium and fine garnet sandpaper, white glue or aliphatic resin (a wood glue). An optional help is a circle-cutting attachment for a ¼-in. electric drill, which makes the job of cutting wheels easier.

Train

	Pattern piece	Quantity	Lumber	Dowels and miscellaneous
Coal car	Side	2	½-in. lumber	**Pull peg:** ½-in. dowel, 1¼-in. long
	Back	1	½-in. lumber	**Axles:** Two ½-in. dowels, each 6-in.
	Bed	1	2-in. lumber	long
	Wheels (large)*	4	¾-in. lumber	
Engine	Cab roof	1	½-in. lumber	**Whistle:** ½-in. dowel, 1¼-in. long
	Cab side	2	½-in. lumber	**Smokestack:** 1-in. dowel, 1¼-in.
	Smokestack platform	1	¼-in. lumber	long, shaped to pattern
	Cab front	1	½-in. lumber	**Lamp:** ½-in. dowel, ½-in. long
	Light	1	¼-in. lumber	**Engine boiler:** 3-in. diameter wood
	Bed	1	2-in. lumber	cylinder, 6½-in. long
	Large wheels*	4	¾-in. lumber	**Axles:** Three ½-in. dowels, each
	Small wheels**	2	¾-in. lumber	4¾-in. long
	Cow catcher	1	2 × 4	**Pull peg:** ½-in. dowel, 1¼-in. long
				Side cylinder: Two 1-in. dowels, 1¾-in. long, flattened on 1 side
Automobile carrier	Upper level	1	½-in. lumber	**Upper Level Auto Holders:** Two
	Side supports	4	½-in. lumber	¼-in. dowels, each 2¾-in. long,
	Bed	1	2-in. lumber	sanded flat on 1 side
	Large wheels*	4	¾-in. lumber	**Axle:** Two ½-in. dowels, each 6¼-in. long
				Pull peg: ½-in. dowel, 1¼-in. long
Autos 1 and 2 (2 autos are alike; assembled separately)	Body	2	¾-in. lumber	**Axles:** Two ¼-in. dowels, each 2-in. long
	Wheels (tiny)	8	1⅜-in. diam. dowel, sliced ½-in. thick drill ¼-in. center hole	

(cont'd.)

Train (cont'd)	Pattern piece	Quantity	Lumber	Dowels and miscellaneous
Limousine	Body	1	¾-in. lumber	**Axles:** Same as auto (above)
	Wheels	4	Same as auto (above)	
Pickup	Body	1	¾-in. lumber	**Axles:** Same as auto (above)
	Wheels	4	Same as auto (above)	
Caboose	Bed	1	2-in. lumber	**Axles:** Two ½-in. dowels, each 6-in. long
	Roof	1	½-in. lumber	
	Side	2	½-in. lumber	
	Upper level	1	2-in. lumber	
	Upper level roof	1	½-in. lumber	
	Large wheels*	4	¾-in. lumber	
	Front and back	2	½-in. lumber	
Passenger car	Side	2	½-in. lumber	**Axles:** Two ½-in. dowels, each 6-in. long
	Bed	1	2-in. lumber	**Pull peg:** One ½-in. dowel, 1¾-in. long
	Large wheels*	4	¾-in. lumber	**Passenger:** Two 1-in. dowels, each 2½-in. long, shaped as pattern
	Roof	1	½-in. lumber	
	Front and back	2	½-in. lumber	
Crane car	Inner body	1	½-in. lumber	**Outer turning peg:** ½-in. dowel, 1½-in. long
	Outer body	2	2-in. lumber	**Inner turning peg:** ½-in. dowel, 4½-in. long
	Lever	1	½-in. lumber	**Bottom swivel dowel:** 1-in. dowel, 4-in. long
	Bed	1	2-in. lumber	**Holding pin:** ¼-in. dowel, 2-in. long
	Swivel base	1	½-in. lumber	**Axles:** Two ½-in. dowels, each 5-in. long
	Large wheels*	4	¾-in. lumber	**Pull peg:** One ½-in. dowel, 1¾-in. long
Freight car	Side	2	½-in. lumber	**Axles:** Two ½-in. dowels, each 6-in. long
	Bed	1	2-in. lumber	
	End	2	½-in. lumber	
	Large wheels	4	¾-in. lumber	

In addition, you need 5 square blocks for the alphabet/number freight blocks, each 2½-in. square.

* Large wheels are 2½-in. in diameter, with ½-in. center holes for axles.
** Small wheels are 2-in. in diameter, with ½-in. center holes for axles.

Although it is not strictly necessary, the wheels will roll more easily if metal washers are added between the wheel and the bed on both sides of an axle.

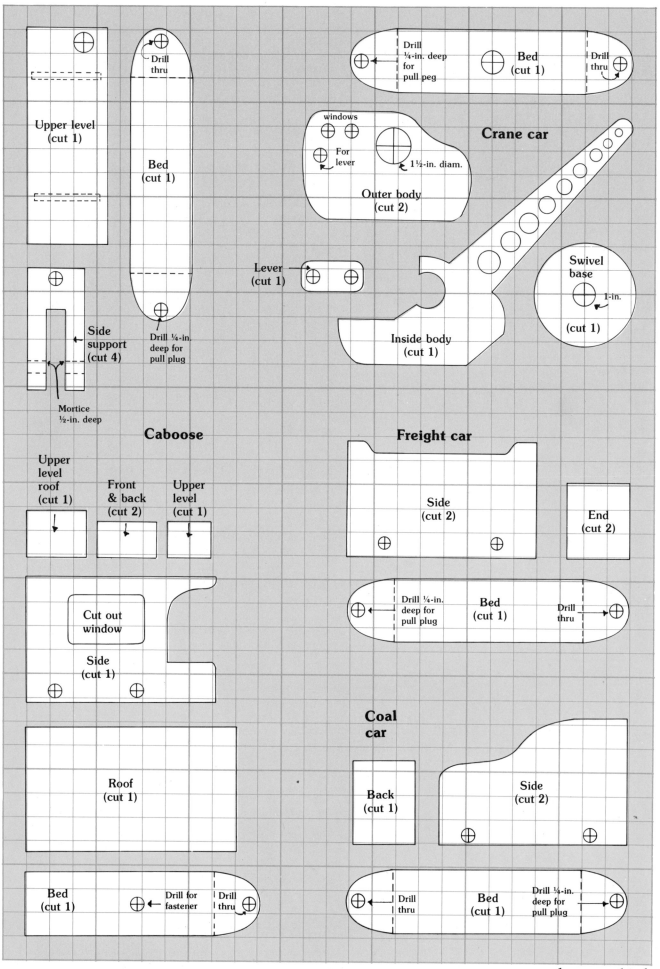

Upper level (cut 1)

Bed (cut 1)

Drill thru

Drill ¼-in. deep for pull peg

Bed (cut 1)

Drill thru

Crane car

windows

For lever

1½-in. diam.

Outer body (cut 2)

Lever (cut 1)

Swivel base

1-in.

(cut 1)

Inside body (cut 1)

Side support (cut 4)

Drill ¼-in. deep for pull plug

Mortice ½-in. deep

Caboose

Upper level roof (cut 1)

Front & back (cut 2)

Upper level (cut 1)

Freight car

Side (cut 2)

End (cut 2)

Cut out window

Side (cut 1)

Bed (cut 1)

Drill ¼-in. deep for pull plug

Drill thru

Coal car

Roof (cut 1)

Back (cut 1)

Side (cut 2)

Bed (cut 1)

Drill for fastener

Drill thru

Drill thru

Bed (cut 1)

Drill ¼-in. deep for pull plug

1 square = 1 inch

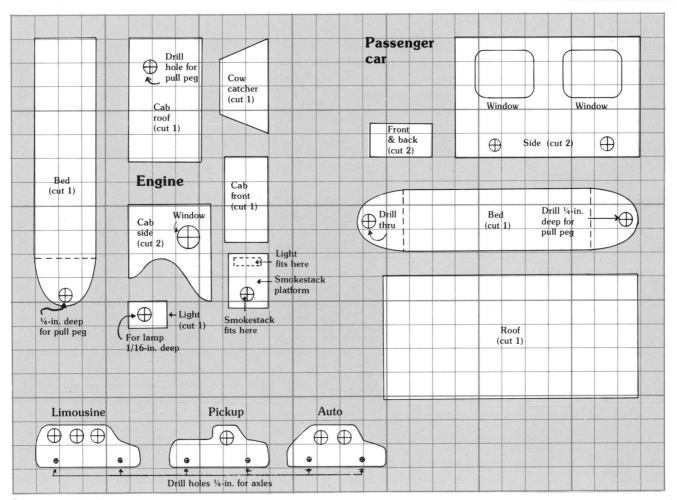

Engine

Bed (cut 1)

1/4-in. deep for pull peg

Drill hole for pull peg

Cab roof (cut 1)

Cab side (cut 2)

Window

For lamp 1/16-in. deep

Light (cut 1)

← Light

Cow catcher (cut 1)

Cab front (cut 1)

Light fits here

Smokestack platform

Smokestack fits here

Passenger car

Window   Window

Front & back (cut 2)   Side (cut 2)

Drill thru   Bed (cut 1)   Drill 1/4-in. deep for pull peg

Roof (cut 1)

Limousine   Pickup   Auto

Drill holes 1/4-in. for axles

1 square = 1 inch

Cutting the pieces

1. Cut out the individual paper pattern pieces for the train car you are building.

2. Follow the directions given on the materials chart, being certain you cut each piece from the correct thickness and type of wood.

Note: In cases where 2 pieces are cut exactly alike (such as the coal car sides) there will be only 1 pattern given. To make 2 pieces exactly alike, tape 2 pieces of wood together with masking tape, draw the pattern onto the top piece of wood, and cut them out at the same time. If the wood is too thick to be cut double, cut 1 piece, and use it as a pattern to cut the remaining piece.

3. Cut the wood carefully along the lines of each pattern.

4. Cut the proper size and number of wooden dowel rods and wheels as indicated on the chart.

Drilling, shaping, and sanding

1. Drill all window cutouts where indicated on the pattern piece; enlarge the bigger windows with a sabre saw. All holes on the pattern pieces are 1/2-in. in diameter, unless otherwise specified.

2. Drill 1/2-in. holes through the exact center of all wheels.

3. In order to connect the train cars, the front and back of adjacent cars must overlap. To accomplish this, each car must be cut out at the front and back (the caboose is cut only at the front; the engine only at the back). Cut away 3/4-in. where indicated (see diagram).

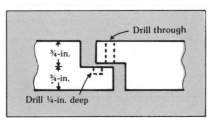

3/4-in.

3/4-in.

Drill through

Drill 1/4-in. deep.

Fig. A. *Drill holes.*

4. Drill ½-in. holes in the front and back of each train car bed as indicated on the pattern pieces.

These holes will later be used to connect the finished cars.

Assembly

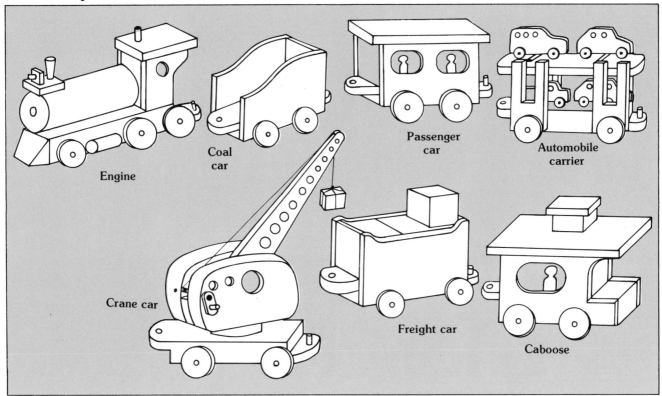

Fig. B. *Assemble train cars.*

1. Thoroughly sand all pieces of wood. Begin with medium sandpaper, and finish with fine.

2. Assemble the train cars as shown, using nails and glue. Any time 2 pieces must be glued only (where nails are not practical), pressure should be applied to the glued joint for several hours.

Engine assembly

a. Saw cow catcher from wide edge to narrow edge as shown in the diagram.

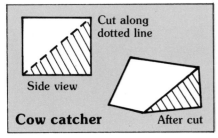

Cow catcher

Fig. C. *Saw cow catcher.*

b. Attach wide edge of cow catcher to front of engine bed.

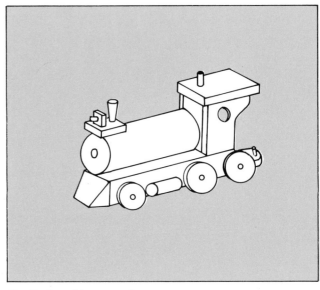

Fig. D. *Assemble cow catcher.*

c. Assemble cab sides, front, roof, and whistle; attach to the rear of the engine.

d. Sand 1 side of engine boiler slightly flat, and glue it in place on the front of the engine bed.

e. Assemble the smokestack platform, smokestack, light, and lamp. Attach the completed unit to the top front of the boiler.

Crane car

This is the only car which is a bit tricky to assemble.

a. Drill window holes in both crane outer body pieces.

b. Drill holes in crane extension on the inner body.

c. Glue inner body between 2 outer bodies.

d. Assemble the crane lever as shown in the diagram.

To secure the inner turning peg, and yet allow it to turn freely, the following steps are taken:

1. With a ¼-in. drill bit, drill into the back left side of the assembled crane body just at the lower edge of the inner turning peg.

2. With a drill still running, manually turn the inner turning peg so that it is grooved inside the crane by the still-running drill (see diag).

3. Insert a piece of ¼-in. dowel into the drilled hole, and sand it flush with the outside edge of the crane body.

4. To attach string, drill a ¼-in. hole through the inner turning peg as shown, insert string through the drilled hole and tie and knot on 1 side. Drill another hole through the top end of the crane extension and thread the free end of the string through that hole. Tie the free end around a wooden block.

e. Drill a 1-in. diameter hole 1-in. deep in the center bottom of assembled crane car body.

f. Assemble swivel mechanism as shown in diagram.

Fig. E. *Assembled crane car.*

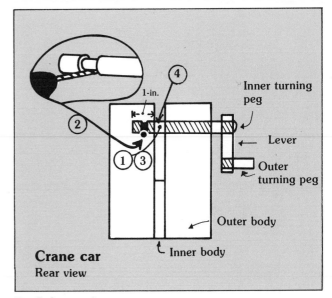

Crane car
Rear view

Fig. F. *Inner turning peg.*

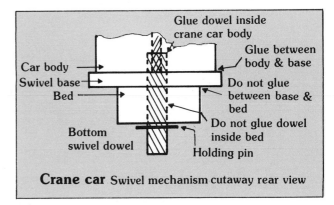

Crane car Swivel mechanism cutaway rear view

Fig. G. *Swivel mechanism.*

Coal car, automobile carrier, passenger car, freight car, and caboose

Assembly

There is no trick to assembling these 5 cars. They are all assembled with the 2 sides fitting on the outside edges of their beds. (See the illustrations.)

Finishing

Drill 2 axle holes through the sides of each of the train cars. The holes should be slightly over ½-in. in diameter to accommodate the ½-in. axle dowels. Use the pattern for approximate location only. Measure each of the holes to make certain they are drilled the same distance from the bottom of the car. The 1 exception is the train engine, which has 3 axle holes. The 2 back axle holes must be drilled higher than the front hole to allow for the larger wheel size on the back. Add the side cylinders to the engine after attaching the wheels.

Adding the wheels

1. Insert the proper length of dowel (axles) through the axle hole.

2. Slip a metal washer onto both ends of each axle dowel.

3. Attach the proper size wheel with a spot of glue. Let the glue set overnight.

DINOSAUR PUZZLES

These wooden toy puzzles are quick, easy, and a real source of delight for our children. We've made a lot of them as gifts for birthday parties which our children attend.

We use scrap wood to make the puzzles. Wood which is 1-in. or 1½-in. is preferable. You can cut them from thinner material, but they do not stand by themselves as well. Also, yellow pine or some kind of hardwood is preferable to a soft wood.

The only tools you'll need are a coping saw, some sandpaper, and a drill and drill bit (for drilling the eyes).

Enlarge the designs shown. Cut the entire puzzle following the outer lines. Drill holes for eyes where indicated. Sand the puzzle to eliminate sharp edges and splinters. Then cut the sanded puzzle into separate parts following the dotted lines.

The finished puzzles can then be painted or stained. As with all children's toys, make sure you use a non-toxic finish. If you prefer a natural wood finish, just rub them with regular vegetable oil.

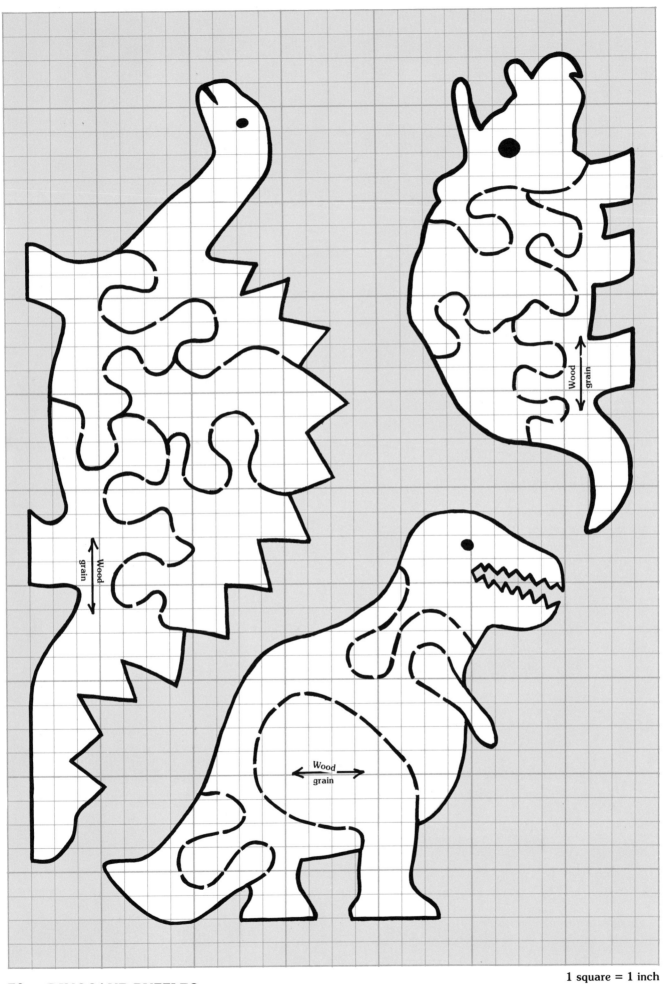

Wood
grain

Wood
grain

Wood
grain

1 square = 1 inch

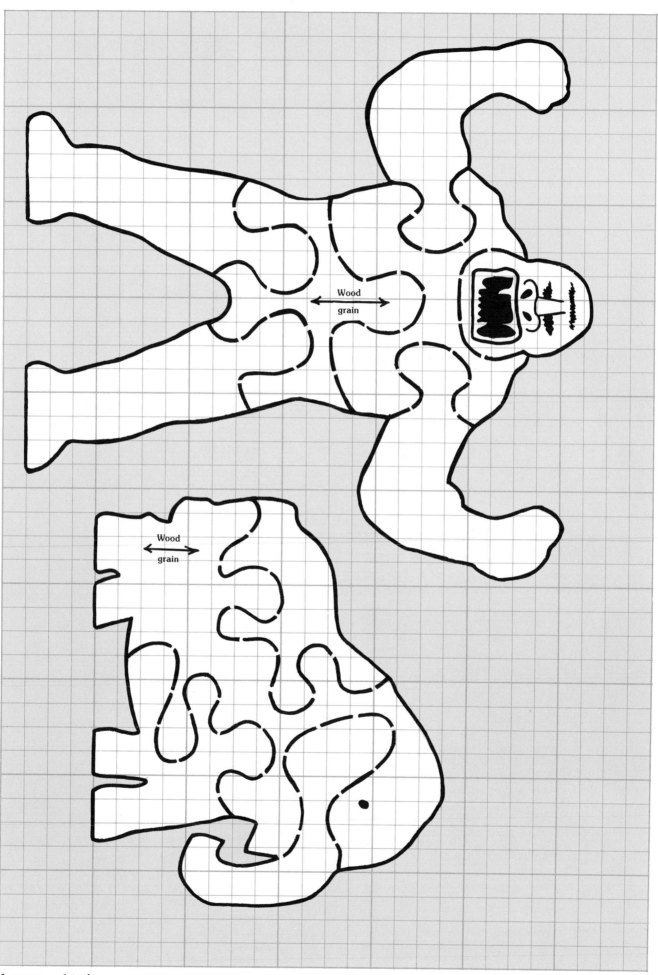

Wood
grain

Wood
grain

1 square = 1 inch

RED BANDANNA STALLION

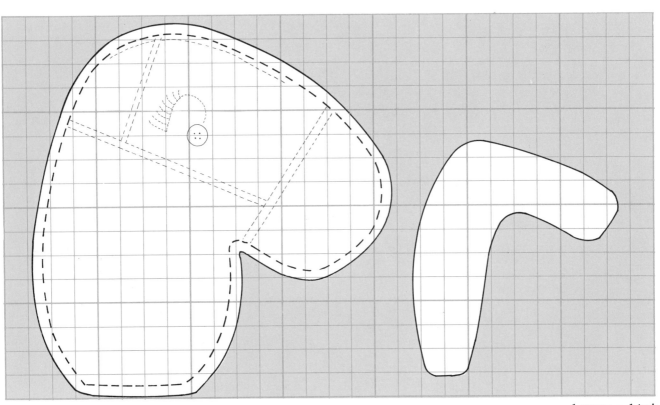

1 square = 1 inch

This project may be made either with only a plain 1-in.-diameter wooden dowel rod; or a wheel, handle and inside head support may be added, depending upon your woodworking abilities and tools.

Materials

½-yd. heavy red bandanna fabric. (If you can find only thin material, either use a double thickness or line it with another fabric).

½-yd. black calico fabric

2 lbs. of polyester fiberfill (or substitute material, such as kapok)

Small amount (about ½ skein) of black embroidery floss and an embroidery needle

Two ¾-in.-diameter black buttons

Wooden dowel rod, 1½-in. in diameter and 22 to 26-in. long, depending upon the size of your child. It can be trimmed later.

1 skein of black rug yarn and needle with eye large enough to accommodate 1 strand of yarn

Scissors and straight pins

For the optional wood parts (wheel, handle and inside head support) you need:

Wooden block, 2-in. × 2-in., 6-in. long

¼-in.-thick plywood, 11½-in. × 10½-in.

Two ½-in.-diameter wooden dowel rods; one 2¼-in. long and one 7-in. long

Small finishing nails

Wood glue (or white glue)

4-in. × 4-in. piece of ¾-in. thick lumber

Tools

Hammer, electric drill with ½-in. and 1-in. drill bits, sabre saw, and sandpaper.

Making the optional wood parts

1. Enlarge and draw the inner head pattern on the ¼-in. plywood and cut out.

2. Cut a ½-in.-wide slot, 2-in. deep into the center of 1 end of the large (1½-in. diameter) wooden dowel rod.

3. Wipe glue inside the slot and slip it over the center of the plywood "neck." Nail in place.

4. Drill a ½-in. hole straight through the large wooden dowel at right angles to the plywood head.

5. Wipe glue on the small dowel (½-in. diameter) and insert it into the hole you just drilled. Use 2 nails to secure it.

6. Cut a ⅞-in.-wide slot, 3¾-in. deep into 1 end of the 2 × 2 block.

7. Drill a 1-in. hole through the 2 × 2, 1¼-in. from the slotted end. Drill across the slot and through the other side.

8. Drill a 1-in. hole, 1½-in. deep into the other end of the 2 × 2 block.

9. Cut a 4-in. diameter circle from the ¾-in.-thick lumber, and drill a ½-in.-diameter hole through its center.

10. Sand all parts to remove any rough edges which might harm a child.

11. To assemble:

   a. Wipe glue on the free end of the large wooden dowel and insert it into the 1-in. hole in the 2 × 2 block, lining up the ⅞-in. slot with the plywood head.

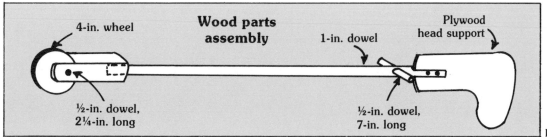

4-in. wheel   **Wood parts assembly**   1-in. dowel   Plywood head support

½-in. dowel, 2¼-in. long   ½-in. dowel, 7-in. long

Fig. A. *Assembly of parts.*

b. Place the wheel into the ⅞-in. slot.

c. Wipe glue on the remaining ½-in. diameter wood dowel (2¼-in. long) and slip it through the side of the block, through the center hole in the wheel, and through the other side of the block.

12. Let the entire project set up overnight so the glue will obtain maximum bond.

Making the head

1. Enlarge the cut 2 head pattern pieces from the red bandanna fabric. Be sure they will match when placed wrong sides together.

2. Sew the button eyes onto the head very securely where indicated on the pattern. 1 button goes on each head piece.

3. Use a full strand of black embroidery floss to embroider the eyelashes on the horse. Embroider both head pieces.

4. Place the 2 head pieces right sides together and double stitch around the outside edges, following the stitching line. Leave the bottom of the neck unstitched for turning and stuffing. You need enough room to comfortably get your hand inside. Double stitch the seam to make sure it is secure.

5. Clip the seams all the way around, and turn the head right side out. Press carefully with an iron.

6. To make the mane, cut 7-in.-long pieces of black rug yarn, thread them through the large-eyed needle, and take 1 stitch through the head along the line for the mane. Remove the needle, pull the 2 ends of the yarn until they are of equal length, and tie the 2 ends in a knot. Add another length of yarn on the opposite side of the head in the same manner. These 2 pieces will form the beginning of 2 rows of the yarn mane.

Continue cutting and adding yarn very closely together in the 2 rows, along the length of the mane guidelines.

Assembly

1. If you have chosen to make the plywood head support, slip it into the fabric head and stuff polyester batting around it until the head is very firm. If you are making the head without the plywood support, stuff the face and top of the head firmly, insert the wooden dowel, and stuff the remaining batting around it.

2. Fold the raw edges of the fabric neck to the inside and whipstitch together by hand, fitting it carefully around the wooden dowel rod.

3. Cut strips of black calico fabric 2-in. wide. You need a total of 9-ft. for the bridle and reins—exact length will depend upon how firm the padding is. Fold the strips right sides together and sew a ¼-in. seam opposite the fold to form a long ¾-in. wide strip.

4. Turn the strip right side out and press. Use these strips to form the bridle. The first strip goes around the nose of the horse; the second, from the front around the back of the horse's head and back to the front. The third strip fits over the top of the horse's head; and the fourth strip, under its neck. Whipstitch the bridle in place over the pattern guidelines so it is secure.

5. The reins on our horse are 44-ins. long. Be sure to secure the reins firmly by sewing in place, as they will bear a lot of strain.

6. The last step is to make the bow for the horse's neck. Cut a piece of black calico 6-ins. wide and 45-ins. long. Fold it in half along the length, and sew a narrow seam down the side opposite the fold. Turn right side out and press with an iron. Turn the edges inside on each of the ends, and topstitch all the way around the bow. Tie in place on the horse's neck. Tack the bow to the bottom of the horse's head to keep it in place.

SUZIE DOLL

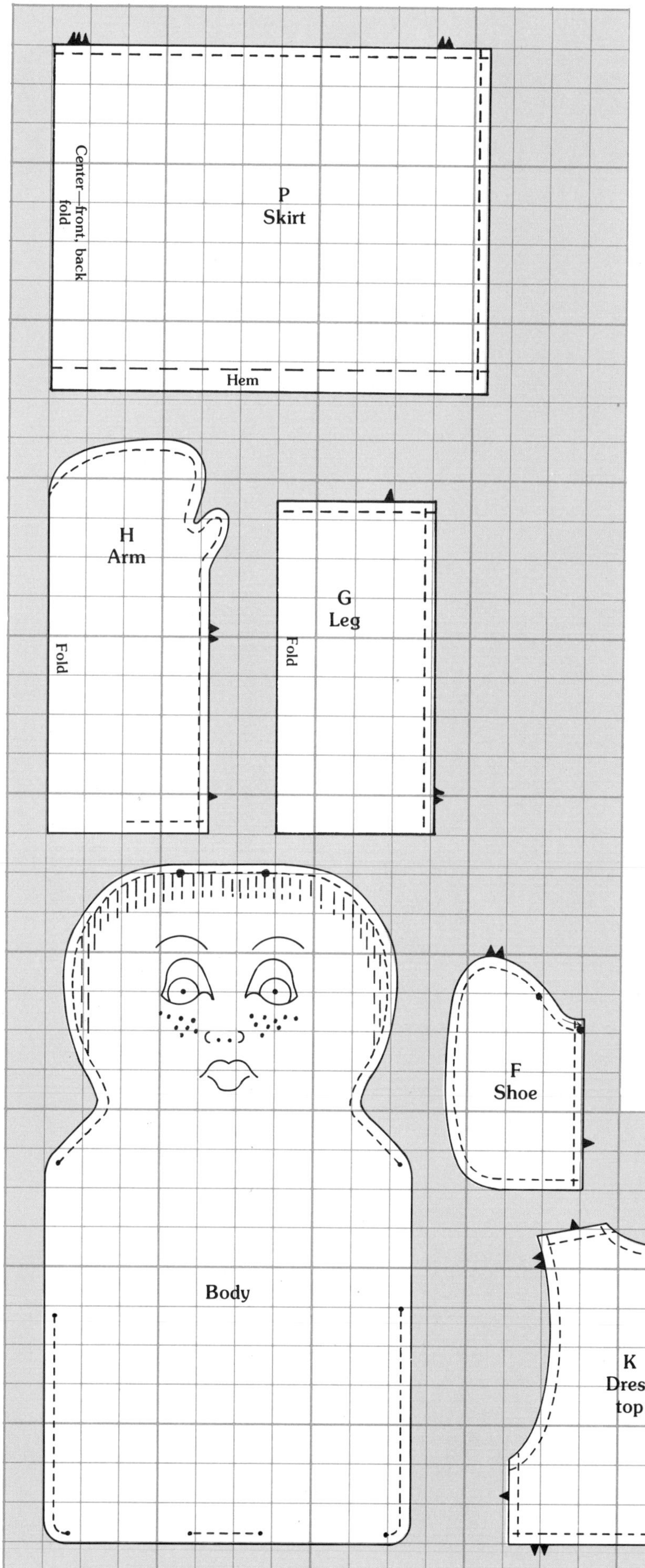

P Skirt

Center—front, back fold

Hem

H Arm

Fold

G Leg

Fold

Body

F Shoe

Note: Cut 4 shoe pieces. Cut 2 of all other pieces.

K Dress top

Fold

M Sleeve

Fold

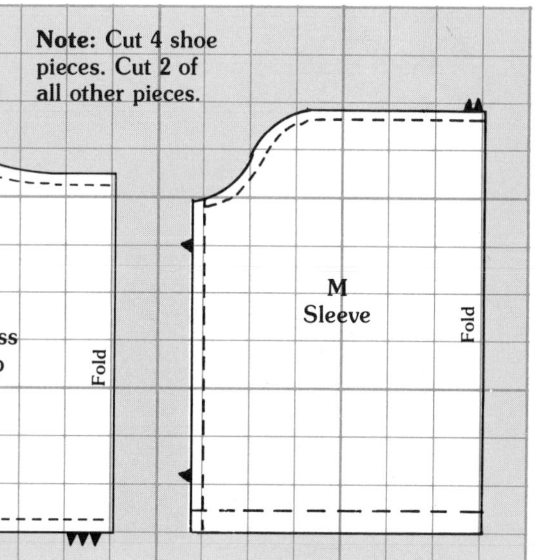

1 square = 1 inch

Materials

Small amounts of scrap fabric for pattern pieces:

White or flesh-colored — body, leg, arm pattern pieces

Bandanna print — sleeve, dress top and skirt, kerchief

Dark print or solid color — shoes

Fiberfill (or kapok) for stuffing

Notions: embroidery thread (blue, brown, pink), large skein of brown rug yarn for hair, large needle, eyelet and rickrack for trim on clothes (optional), small snap, straight pins, needle, thread to match fabrics, scissors, and iron.

Note: When cutting patterns, pay particular attention to "Place on fold" notations, and be sure to cut the number of pattern pieces specified.

Body

1. Place right sides of body together. Sew along seam allowance, leaving openings for legs, arms, and between •'s at top of head.

2. Clip curves, turn right side out and press, turning seam allowances to inside.

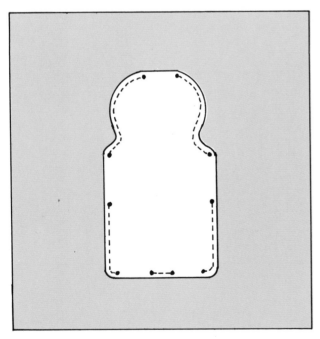

Fig. A. *Sides of body.*

Shoes and legs

1. Sew 2 shoe pieces (F), right sides together between •'s.

Fig. B. *Shoe pieces.*

2. Matching A's, sew bottom of leg to top of shoe placing center shoe seam in center of leg.

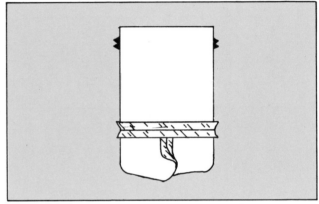

Fig. C. *Sew bottom of leg to top of shoe.*

3. Fold leg right sides together and sew down the back of leg and around shoe. Leave top of leg open.

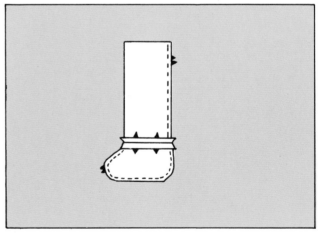

Fig. D. *Fold and sew leg.*

4. Clip curves, turn right side out and press.

5. Stuff with fiberfill.

Arm

1. Sew arm (H) right sides together along side seam and hand.

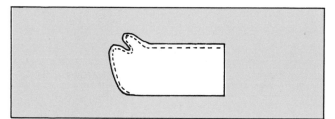

Fig. E. *Sew arm.*

2. Clip curves, turn right side out and press.

3. Repeat for other arm.

4. Stuff both arms with fiberfill.

Finishing body

1. Pin arms (thumbs up) in arm openings on body. Topstitch in place.

Fig. F. *Finish body.*

2. Press top of leg so toe points to front and seam is at center back.

3. Pin legs (toes to front) in leg openings on body. Topstitch in place.

4. Stuff body and head and whipstitch top of head together.

5. Embroider eyes (blue), nose (black), mouth (pink), and freckles (brown). Use the satin stitch.

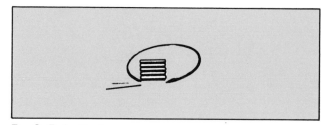

Fig. G. *Embroider face.*

6. Attach hair along dashes and on back of head. Thread needle, pull through fabric, and tie. For long hair, leave both tie ends long; for short hair, cut them to desired length.

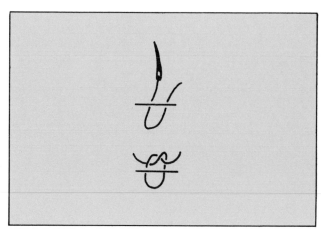

Fig. H. *Attach hair.*

Dress

1. Place dress tops (K) right sides together and sew shoulder seams. Slit center back and hem raw edges of the slit. Turn the raw edges around the neck to the inside and topstitch. Add rickrack to neck and 2 rows down the front of the dress top if desired. Sew snap at neckline in back.

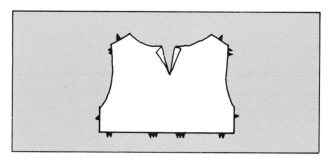

Fig. I. *Sew dress top.*

2. Gather top of sleeve (M) and sew (right sides together) to open armhole, easing to fit.

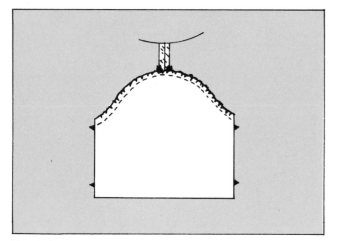

Fig. J. *Sew sleeves.*

3. Hem bottom of sleeve and add rickrack if you wish.

4. Sew underarm and side seams.

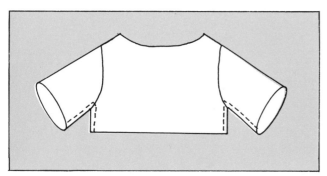

Fig. K. *Attach sleeves to top.*

5. Sew 2 skirt pieces together at side seams.

6. Turn up hem allowance on skirt and stitch. Add lace if desired.

7. Gather skirt along top gathering line.

8. Matching A's (right sides together) sew skirt to dress top, easing gathers to fit.

Kerchief

1. Cut a fabric square, 20 × 20 in.

2. Hem all 4 edges.

3. Fold the square corner to corner forming a triangle.

4. Tie the kerchief around the doll's head.

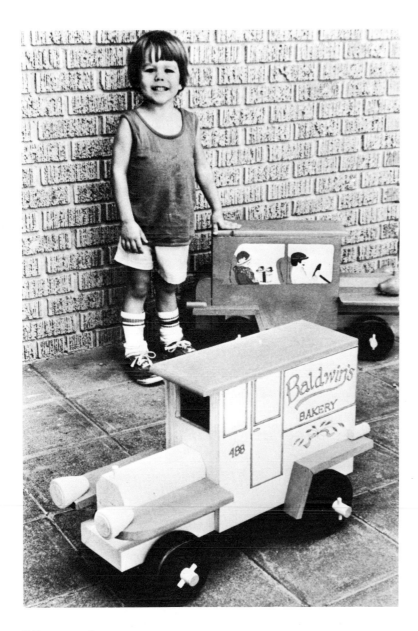

RIDING CAR AND TRUCK

Materials

Lumber	Quantity
1 × 12	3 ft.
2 × 4	4 ft.
2 × 6	3 ft.
2 × 8	7-in.
¾-in. plywood	24 × 16¼-in.
1-in. dowel	3 ft.
⅜-in. dowel	1 ft.
Glue, nails, sandpaper	

Tools

Hammer, saw, carpenter's square, drill.

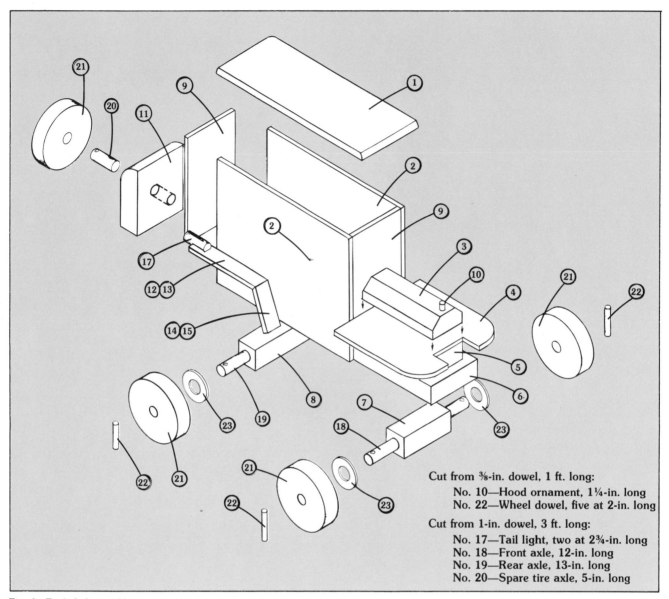

Cut from ⅜-in. dowel, 1 ft. long:
    No. 10—Hood ornament, 1¼-in. long
    No. 22—Wheel dowel, five at 2-in. long

Cut from 1-in. dowel, 3 ft. long:
    No. 17—Tail light, two at 2¾-in. long
    No. 18—Front axle, 12-in. long
    No. 19—Rear axle, 13-in. long
    No. 20—Spare tire axle, 5-in. long

Fig. A. *Exploded assembly.*

Assembly

Both the passenger car and bakery truck are assembled in the same manner and require the same pieces, with the following exceptions noted below:

	Bakery truck	**Passenger car**
Headlights	Mounted to overhang the front fender.	Mounted flush with front fender.
Trunk	Has no trunk.	Trunk is added.
Front panel	Front window is cut out.	No cut-out for window.

There may be other additions you'll wish to make to your truck or car.

Use glue and nails for all assembly operations. Refer to the exploded assembly diagram. It is easier to pre-sand component parts before final assembly.

1. Nail side panels (2) and front and back panels (9) onto the body base (6). Attach top (1).

2. Attach hood (3), front fender (4), motor mount (5), hood ornament (10), and headlights (optional) to body base (6).

3. Add front and back axle supports (7 and 8), axles (18 and 19), and 4 wheels. Place spacers between axle support and wheel. Secure wheels with axle dowels.

4. Add fenders (12, 13, 14, and 15), and tail lights (17).

5. Add (optional) trunk (11), and spare tire.

Adding decorative touches

You can use the designs provided, or personalize the bakery truck name by using your child's first or last name. Paint the truck and car with bright non-toxic paints in the colors of your choice.

Number	Quantity	Description
1	1	Top
2	2	Side panels
3	1	Hood
4	1	Front fender
5	1	Motor mount
6	1	Body base
7	1	Axle support (front)
8	1	Axle support (rear)
9	2	Front and back panel
10	1	Hood ornament
11	1	Rear trunk
12 & 13	1 ea.	Rear fenders (top)
14 & 15	1 ea.	Rear fenders (front)
16	2	Headlights (optional)
17	2	Tail light
18	1	Front axle
19	1	Rear axle
20	1	Spare tire axle
21	5	Wheel
22	5	Wheel dowel
23	4	Spacers

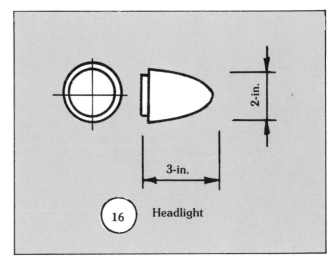

Fig. B. *Headlight.*

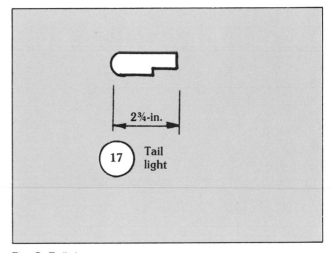

Fig. C. *Taillight.*

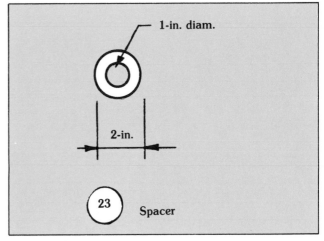

Fig. D. *Spacer.*

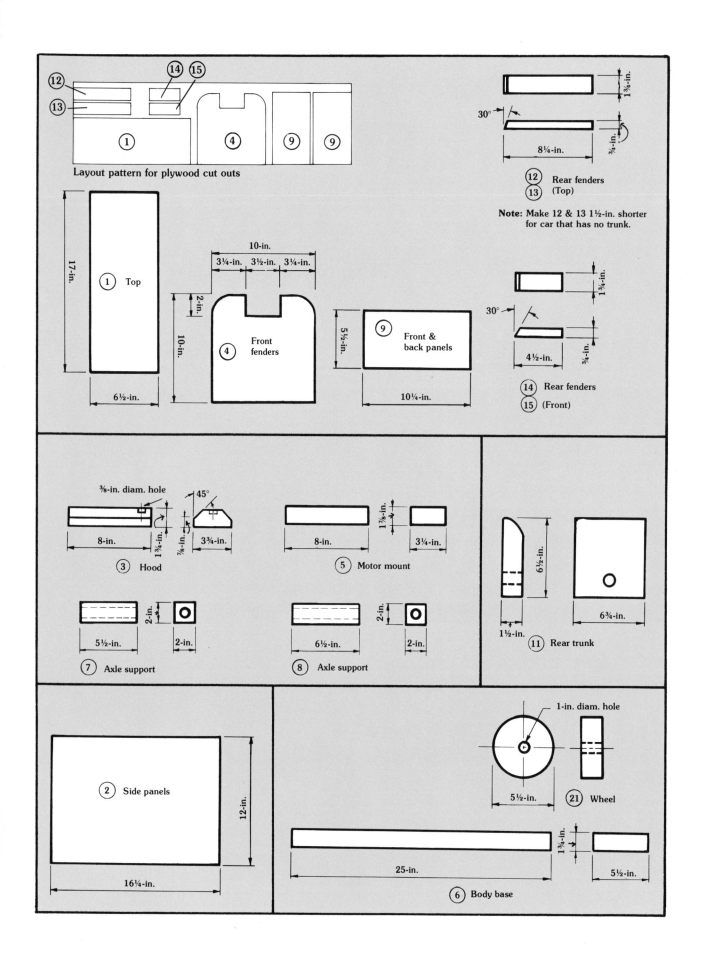

Layout pattern for plywood cut outs

⑫ ⑬ Rear fenders (Top)

Note: Make 12 & 13 1½-in. shorter for car that has no trunk.

① Top

④ Front fenders

⑨ Front & back panels

⑭ ⑮ Rear fenders (Front)

③ Hood

⑤ Motor mount

⑪ Rear trunk

⑦ Axle support

⑧ Axle support

② Side panels

㉑ Wheel

⑥ Body base

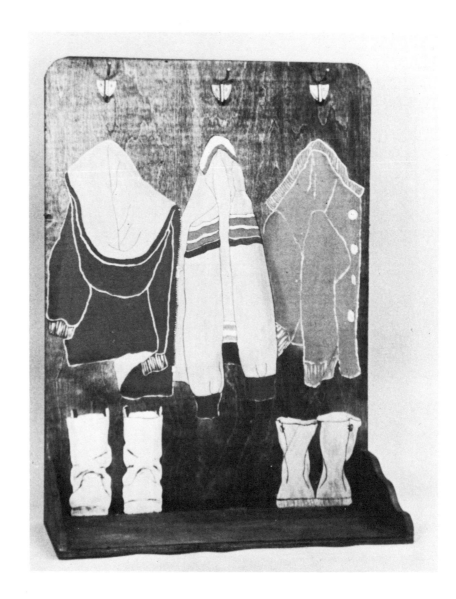

COATRACK

Materials

Pegged Coatrack: 1 × 8 lumber, 21-in. long
4 wooden shaker pegs
acrylic paints (black, white, blue, orange, yellow)

Standing Coatrack: ¾-in.-thick plywood, 4 × 4 ft.
3 metal coat hooks with screws
wood stain
acrylic paints (black, blue, green, orange, white, and yellow)

Tools

Circular saw, sabre saw, router, drill, screwdriver, hammer, nails, wood glue and sandpaper.

Assembly

Pegged coatrack:

1. Cut the 1 × 8 lumber to 21 × 7-in. Rout the edges (optional).

2. Drill holes to fit the size of the shaker pegs.

3. Sand thoroughly, beginning with medium and ending with fine sandpaper.

4. Enlarge and transfer the baseball design onto the board, centering the pattern.

5. Paint the design following the coded illustration, and letter your child's name on the cap. Paint the board and pegs yellow.

6. Wipe glue onto the end of the shaker pegs, and insert in the drilled holes.

7. Allow the glue to set up overnight.

Standing coatrack

1. Cut the plywood into 4 pieces having the following dimensions:
   Back—36 × 26-in.
   Bottom—26 × 9½-in.
   2 Side supports—9½- by 9½-in. cut triangles. Add a curve if you wish

2. Sand the pieces, beginning with coarse and ending with fine sandpaper.

3. Enlarge and transfer the coat and boot pattern onto the back piece. Paint the design following the coded illustration.

4. Assemble the 4 pieces according to the diagram, using wood glue and nails.

5. Stain the entire coatrack. An oil stain will not adhere to acrylic paints.

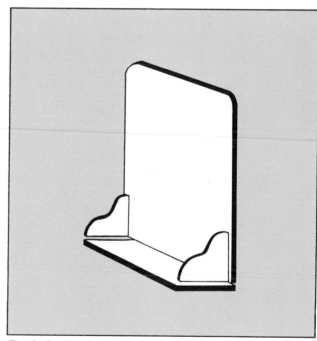

Fig. A. *Back, bottom and sides of coatrack.*

6. Attach the hooks at the top of the coatrack as shown in the picture.

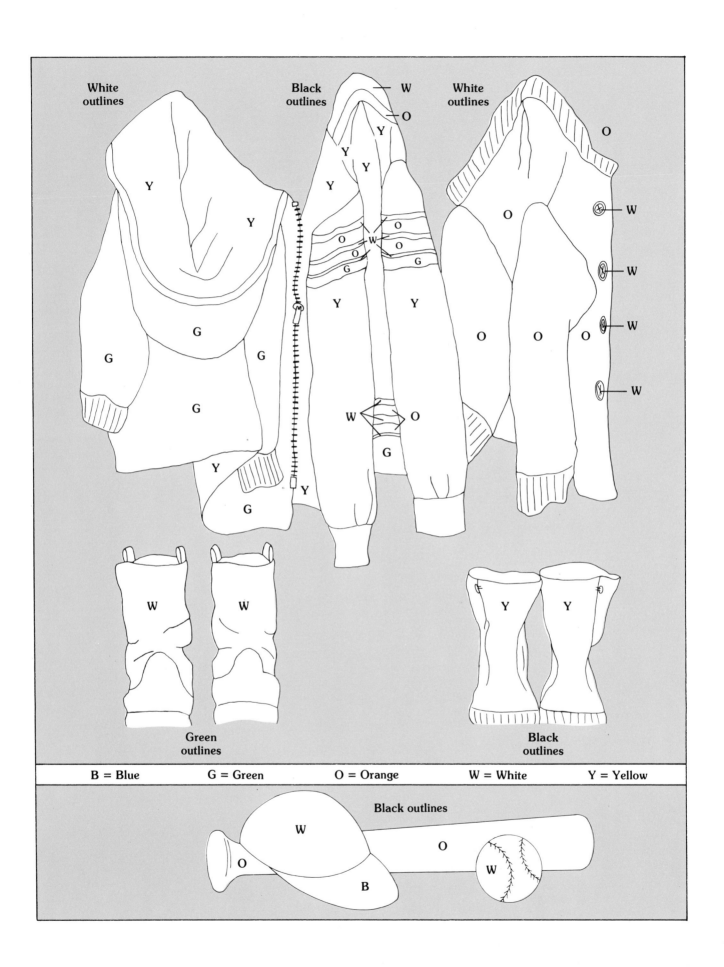

POLKA DOT UNICORN

Materials

4 × 8-ft. sheet of ¾-in. plywood (⅜- or ½-in. may also be used)
1 in.-diameter wooden dowel rod, 8-in. long
Finishing nails, 1¼-in. long
2 × 8 lumber, 4 ft. long (for the rockers)
Wood glue
Rough and medium sandpaper sheets
Wood filler (optional) to cover all nail holes
7 × 15-in. piece of leather (for ears)
1 ft. length of rope for tail
Non-toxic paint and brush (The colors we used are listed under "Finishing", but any color may
   be changed according to your preference.)

Tools

Ruler, hammer.
Sabre saw (or coping saw).
Nailset to recess nails (a large nail will substitute).
Drill with 1-in. spade drill bit.
Router with corner-round bit (optional).

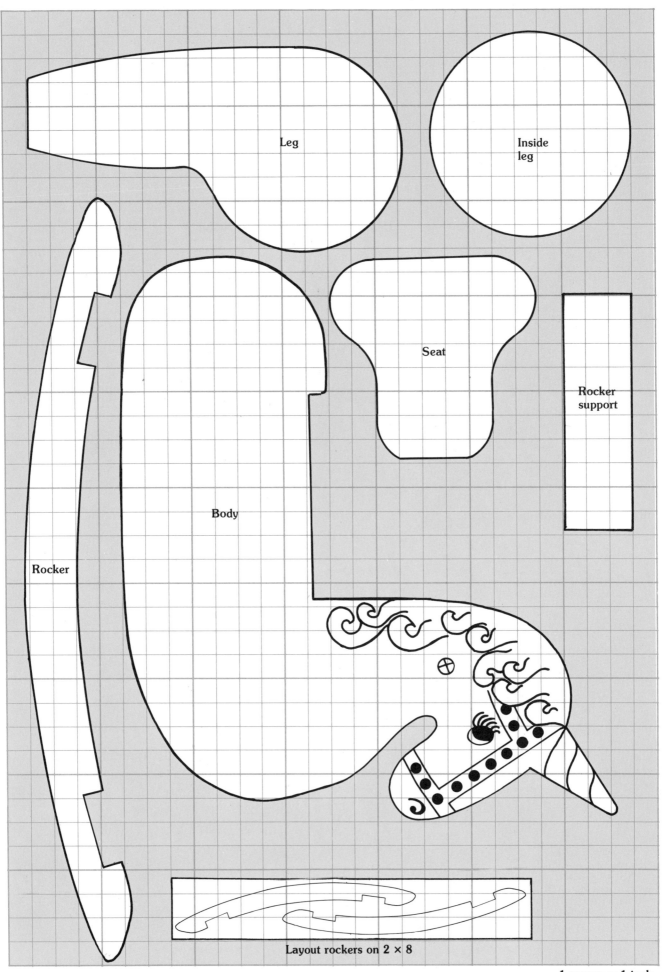

Leg

Inside
leg

Seat

Rocker
support

Body

Rocker

Layout rockers on 2 × 8

1 square = 1 inch

Enlarging the patterns

Each square of the printed design represents 1-in. To enlarge the design to life-size, follow these steps:

1. Mark off the 4 × 8-ft. piece of plywood into 1-in. squares corresponding to the number of squares on the printed chart.

2. Copy the outline from the printed chart to the plywood squares, 1 square at a time.

Cutting, drilling and sanding

1. There are 14 cutting pieces: 2 each of the body (A), rocker (C), rocker support (E), and 4 each of the leg (B), and inside leg (D). Cut 1 of each piece, and use it to cut the additional pieces required. You need cut only 1 seat (F).

2. Sand each of the pieces individually. Use coarse sandpaper first, and finish with medium.

3. Drill a 1-in. hole through the head where indicated on the pattern to accommodate the wooden dowel rod handle which will be added later.

4. An optional step at this point is to use a router to round all edges of the rockers, body, seat, and legs.

Assembly

1. Glue and nail the body pieces together.

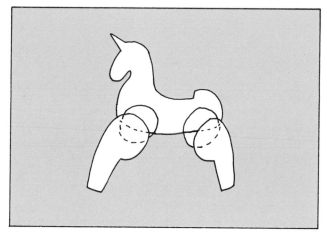

Fig. A. *Assembly.*

2. Connect the rockers by attaching the rocker supports to the front and back.

3. To make certain that the legs and inside legs are evenly attached to the rocker supports, we suggest you perform a temporary assembly; drive a nail through the leg and inside leg and into the body. Adjust the legs to fit securely against the rocker supports.

4. After you have determined that the rocking action is smooth and even, remove the nails and assemble permanently with glue and nails.

5. Lastly, insert the wood dowel rod through the hole in the head and secure it with a dab of glue.

Finishing

Paint the unicorn following the pattern (consult the photo for placement of the polka dots). Use a non-toxic paint. We painted the body yellow, the mane and polka dots brown, the eyes blue (with black lashes) and the bridle red.

Cut leather ears as shown in the diagram, then fold and nail them to each side of the painted head.

Unravel 1 end of the rope, and nail the other end to the unicorn as shown in the photograph.

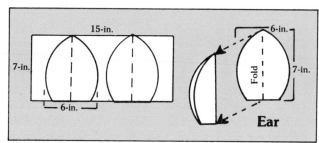

Fig. B. *Leather ears.*

SOURPUSS LION AND GRINNING GIRAFFE

The body design for both these rocking toys is identical—only the head is different. This allows you to conjure up many designs for the head besides the giraffe and lion which are provided. You might want to also try a turtle, snail, horse, elephant, etc.

Materials

Lumber for *each* body: 4 ft. length of 2 × 8 lumber
5½ ft. length of 2 × 6 lumber
4 ft. length of 1 × 6 lumber

Materials for the head: **Giraffe:**
3 ft. length of 2 × 12 lumber
2 wooden shaker pegs approximately 3-in. long with ½-in. diameter ends (or substitute wooden dowel rods)
Soft leather or heavy canvas fabric 18 × 5 in.

Lion:
2 ft. length of 2 × 12 lumber
Approximately 20 yds. of 3-ply No. 72 jute (or substitute any jute or a rope approximately ¼-in. in diameter)

In addition, you need a small amount of black acrylic paint and a small paint brush for painting the facial features, a sabre saw, ten 2-in. long wood screws (a total of 20 for both toys), a 16-in. length of ½-in.-diameter rope for each animal tail, wood glue, and sandpaper (both medium and fine). Each rocking toy also takes a 7-in. length of 1-in.-diameter wooden dowel rod for the handle. You'll also need a drill and drill bits for the holes marked ⊕ on the pattern.

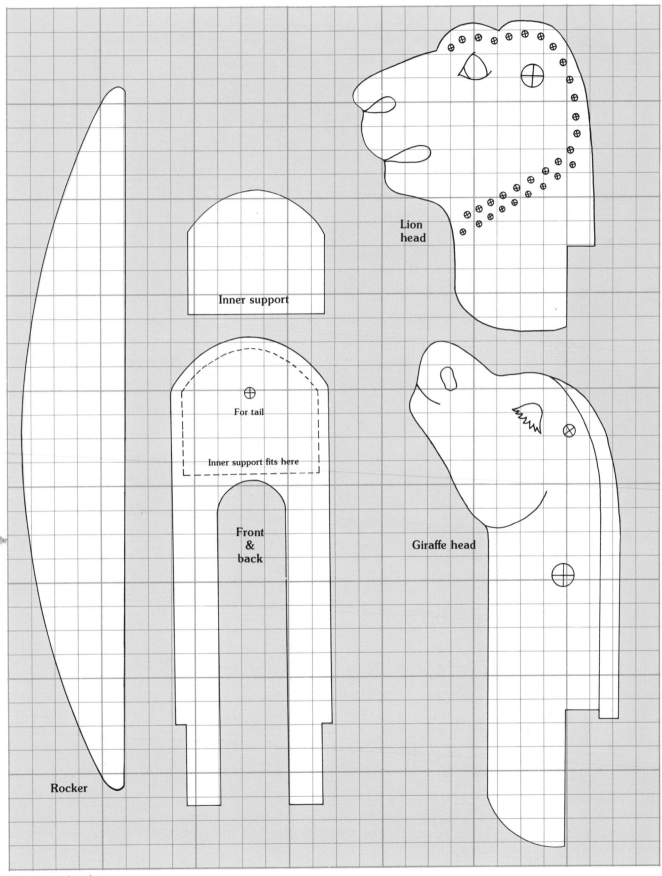

Lion
head

Inner support

For tail

Inner support fits here

Front
&
back

Giraffe head

Rocker

1 square = 1 inch

Cut the following pieces:

Code	Quantity	Description	Type of Lumber
A	2	Front and back (forequarters and hindquarters)	2 × 8 lumber
B	2	Inner support	1 × 6 lumber or plywood
C	2	Rockers	2 × 6 lumber
	13	Slats, each 14-in. long, ¾ × ¾-in.	1-in. lumber
	1	Handle, 7-in. long 1-in.-diameter dowel rod	

And the head you choose:

Code	Quantity	Description	Type of Lumber
D	1	Giraffe head	2 × 12 lumber
E	1	Lion head	2 × 12 lumber

Assembly

The following directions apply to both the Giraffe and Lion:

1. Drill holes where indicated on the patterns by ⊕'s.

2. Nail and glue the inner supports to the inside of the front and back pieces, aligning them with the dotted lines on the pattern.

3. Connect the front and back by nailing the 13 slats onto the edges of the inner supports. Center and nail one slat to the top of the inner supports. Then evenly space the remaining 12 slats—6 slats on each side of the center slat.

4. Attach the rockers to each side of the assembled body; center the legs on each of the rockers. Use glue and wood screws.

Fig. A. *Assembly.*

5. Attach the head to the center top of the front (A). Use glue and wood screws.

Finishing

Giraffe:

1. Paint the eyes, nose, mouth, and mane black, and add random black spots on the neck and body (see picture).

2. Cut ears from soft leather following the pattern. Poke 1 ear through the hole in the giraffe's head, and pull the ear through.

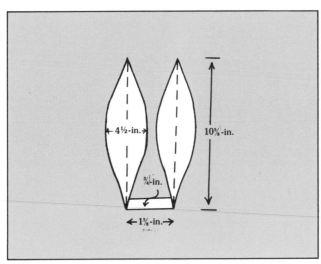

Fig. B. *Giraffe ears.*

Lion:

1. Cut a length of jute (or rope) 2 ft. long. Thread it through the hole closest to the neck front, and pull the ends even. Tie a knot at the neck front.

2. Cut a second 2 ft. length and thread through the second hole and even the ends. Then tie a knot onto the first loop on each side of the head. Repeat for each hole.

3. To fill out the mane, tie additional 2 ft. lengths of jute to the pieces you just tied through the holes. To finish, untwist the jute to make it look fluffy.

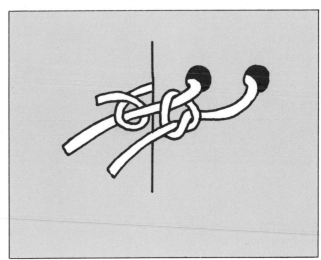

Fig. C. *Lion's mane.*

4. Glue the 16-in. tail in place and untwist the end.

SWINGING HORSE

Materials

18-in. length of 1-in.-diameter wooden dowel rod
⅝-in. exterior grade plywood, one 4 × 8 ft. sheet
2 × 8 hardwood, 3 ft. long
Three 1-in.-diameter bolts, each 6-in. long
1 U-bolt 3-in. wide, with nuts and bar to fit (see illustration)
One large S-hook
Ski rope to hang the finished horse
Finishing nails, masking tape
½-in.-diameter dowel pins for reinforcing the assembly

Tools

Drill, hammer, sandpaper, paint, two C-clamps, scissors.

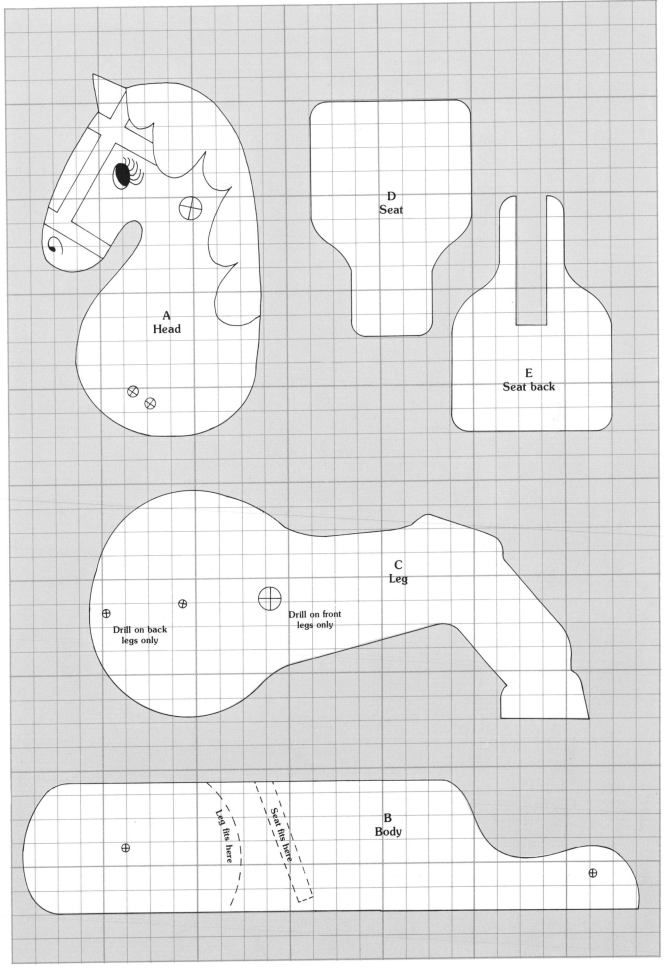

D
Seat

A
Head

E
Seat back

C
Leg

Drill on front
legs only

Drill on back
legs only

B
Body

Leg fits here

Seat fits here

1 square = 1 inch

Cutting, drilling and sanding

1. There are 5 pieces: (A) head, (B) body, (C) legs, (D) seat, and (E) seat back. The head, legs, seat, and seat back are all cut from ⅝-in. exterior plywood. The body (B) is cut from the 2 × 8 piece of hardwood. You also need 2 blocks which will later fit between the bottom legs. Each block is a 2-in. square cut from the 2 × 8 hardwood.

2. Enlarge the pattern pieces and draw each one on the specified lumber. Cut 1 body, 2 heads, 4 legs, 1 seat, 1 seat back, and 2 blocks. After you have cut 1 head, use that cut piece as a pattern to cut the second. Glue the 2 head pieces together. Clamp and let dry.

3. Drill all holes as shown on the patterns. The holes for the wooden dowel rods are 1-in. in diameter, and the holes for the bolts are ⅜-in. in diameter. The hole at the top of the head for the U-bolt attachment is slightly over ⅝-in. in diameter.

Assembly

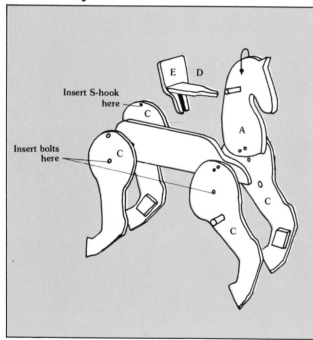

Fig. A. *Assembly.*

1. Glue the 2-in. square blocks in place to support the bottom legs as shown in the assembly illustration.

2. Glue, nail, and dowel the head between the 2 front legs as shown in the illustration. Clamp and set aside to dry.

3. Bolt the 2 back legs to the body as shown in the illustration. Do not use glue in this assembly.

4. Insert another bolt through the top of the back legs. Insert the bolt through 1 leg, slip an S-hook over the bolt, then insert the bolt through the other leg. Add the nut, and tighten.

5. Bolt the head and front leg assembly to the front of the body. Again, use no glue, so the legs can swing freely.

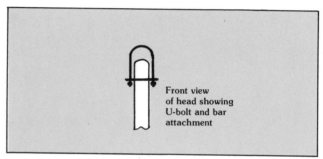

Fig. B. *Handle and footrest.*

6. The seat back fits onto the body at an angle (shown on the body piece pattern). Glue and nail the seat back in place. Then place the seat in front of the seat back. It must be cut at an angle so that it fits flush against the seat back. Nail and glue the seat back in place.

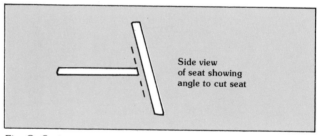

Fig. C. *Seat.*

7. Cut the 18-in. dowel rod in half. Glue one 9-in. piece in the head where indicated for a handle, and the remaining dowel piece through the legs for a footrest. The footrest position may be adjusted to accommodate the size of the child.

Finishing

Sand any remaining rough spots. Paint the finished horse with a good outdoor paint. We painted our horse a bright orange and added a black mane, facial features, and hooves.

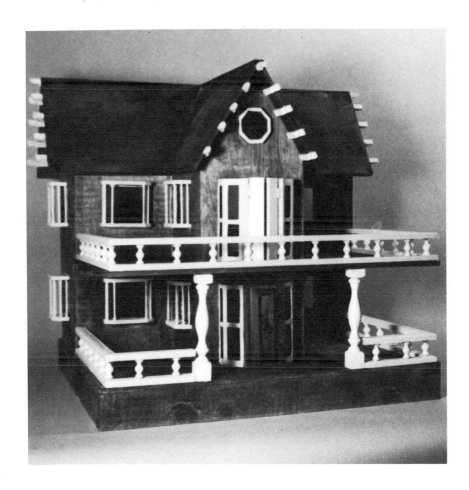

MANSION DOLLHOUSE

Materials

If you position and cut the pieces carefully two 4 × 8 sheets of ⅜-in. thick plywood will be enough. All the pattern pieces (A through Z) are cut from plywood with the exception of W (decorative beam) which are cut from 1-in. lumber.

In addition, you will need the following materials and tools:

72 Wooden dowel rods, ¼-inch in diameter and 4-in. long
4 Small metal hinges
2 Wood turnings for the front porch posts, approximately 9-in. long
A total of 18 ft. of ½-in.-wide strips cut from ⅜-in.-thick plywood (for support strips)
A total of 12 ft. of ready-made decorative railing for the front porch and balcony trim
You will also need a box of small finishing nails, a hammer, saw, carpenter's glue, sandpaper, and a metal square.

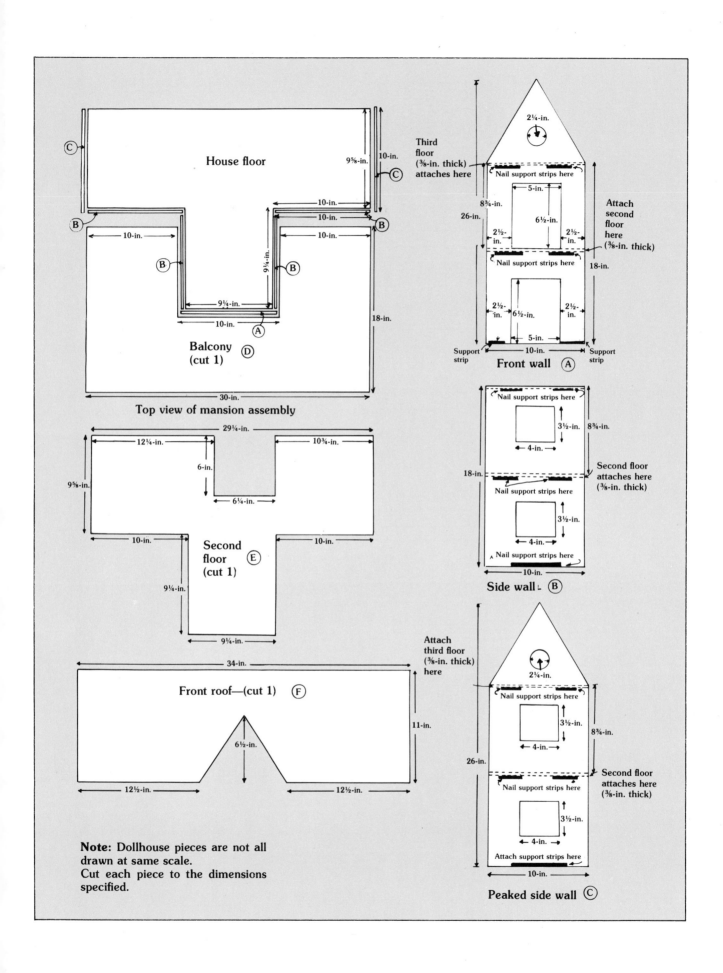

House floor

©

9⅝-in.

10-in.

©

10-in.

10-in.

©

10-in.

B

B

10-in.

9¼-in.

9¼-in.

B

B

9¼-in.

10-in.

A

18-in.

Balcony
(cut 1) D

30-in.

Top view of mansion assembly

Third
floor
(⅜-in. thick)
attaches here

2¼-in.

Nail support strips here

8¾-in.

5-in.

26-in.

6½-in.

Attach
second
floor
here
(⅜-in. thick)

2½-in.

2½-in.

Nail support strips here

18-in.

2½-
in.

6½-in.

2½-
in.

Support
strip

5-in.

10-in.

Support
strip

Front wall A

29¼-in.

12¼-in.

10¾-in.

6-in.

9⅝-in.

6¼-in.

10-in.

10-in.

Second
floor
(cut 1) E

9¼-in.

9¼-in.

Nail support strips here

3½-in.

8¾-in.

4-in.

18-in.

Second floor
attaches here
(⅜-in. thick)

Nail support strips here

3½-in.

4-in.

Nail support strips here

10-in.

Side wall ∟ B

34-in.

Front roof—(cut 1) F

11-in.

6½-in.

12½-in.

12½-in.

Note: Dollhouse pieces are not all
drawn at same scale.
Cut each piece to the dimensions
specified.

Attach
third floor
(⅜-in. thick)
here

2¼-in.

Nail support strips here

3½-in.

8¾-in.

4-in.

26-in.

Second floor
attaches here
(⅜-in. thick)

Nail support strips here

3½-in.

4-in.

Attach support strips here

10-in.

Peaked side wall ©

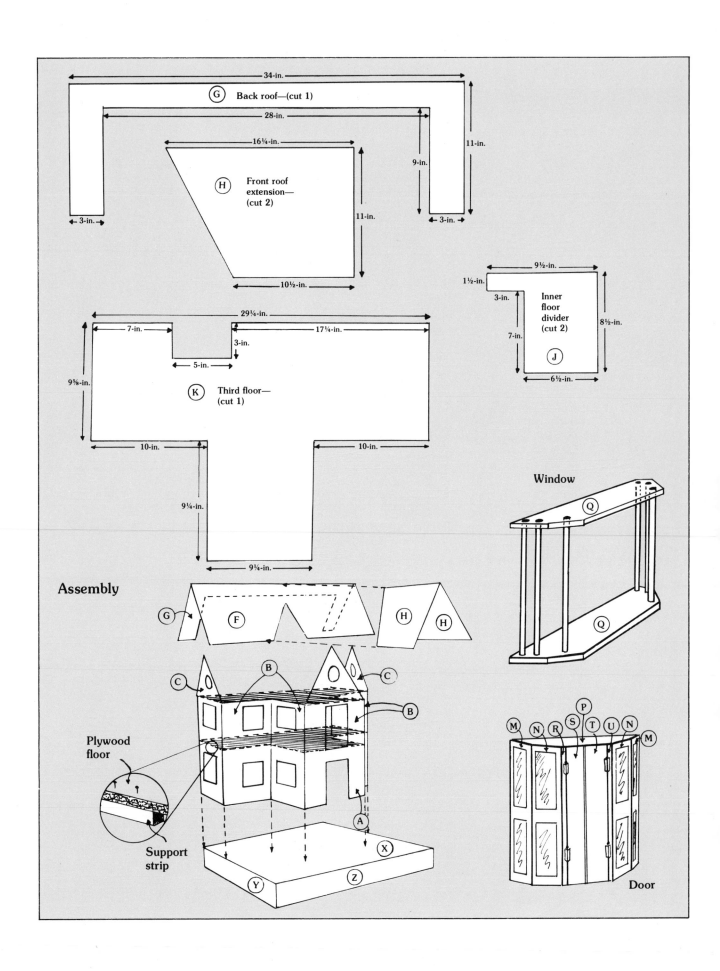

34-in.

G Back roof—(cut 1)

28-in.

11-in.

16¼-in.

9-in.

H Front roof extension—(cut 2)

11-in.

3-in.

3-in.

10½-in.

9½-in.

1½-in.

3-in.

Inner floor divider (cut 2)

8½-in.

7-in.

J

6½-in.

29¼-in.

7-in.

17¼-in.

3-in.

5-in.

9⅝-in.

K Third floor—(cut 1)

10-in.

10-in.

9¼-in.

9¼-in.

Window

Q

Q

Assembly

G F H H

B

C B

C

Plywood floor

Support strip

B

A

X

Y

Z

M N R S P T U N M

Door

MANSION DOLLHOUSE · 99

List of pieces for Mansion Dollhouse

Code	Qty.	Description
A	1	Front wall
B	4	Side wall
C	2	Peaked side wall
D	1	Balcony
E	1	Second floor
F	1	Front roof
G	1	Back roof
H	2	Front roof extension
J	2	Inner floor divider
K	1	Third floor
M	4	Door rear panel
N	4	Door middle panel
P	4	Door top & bottom
Q	24	Window top & bottom
R	2	Left door frame
S	2	Left front door
T	2	Right front door
U	2	Right door frame
V	3	Top window frame
W	27	Decorative beam
X	1	Base
Y	2	Side base support
Z	2	Front & back base support

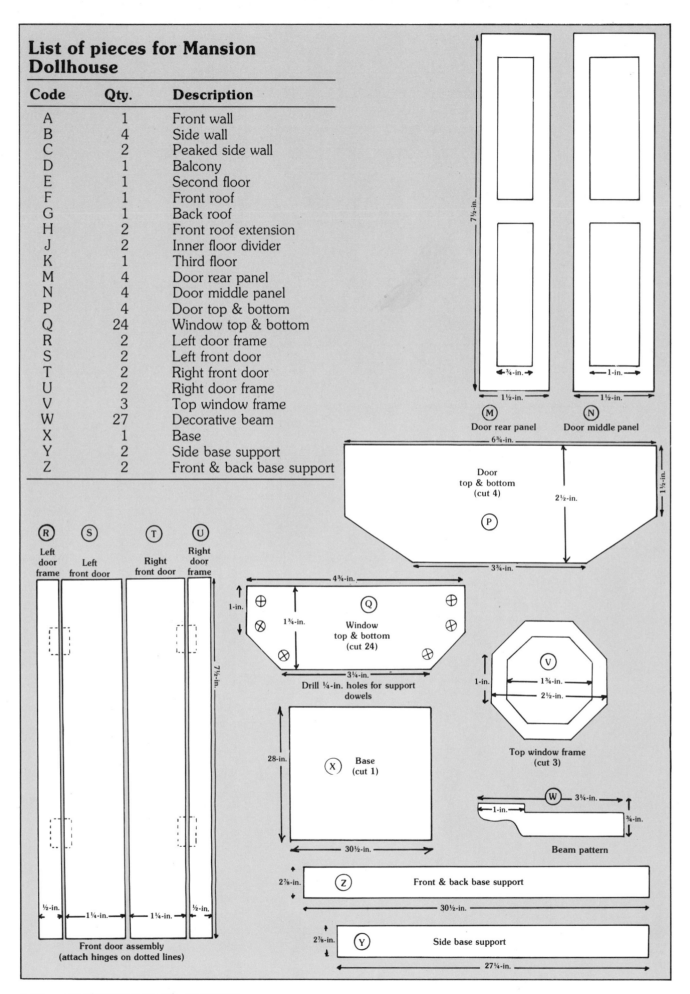

(M) Door rear panel

(N) Door middle panel

Door top & bottom (cut 4) (P)

(R) Left door frame
(S) Left front door
(T) Right front door
(U) Right door frame

Front door assembly
(attach hinges on dotted lines)

Window top & bottom (cut 24) (Q)

Drill ¼-in. holes for support dowels

(X) Base (cut 1)

(V) Top window frame (cut 3)

(W) Beam pattern

(Z) Front & back base support

(Y) Side base support

Assembly

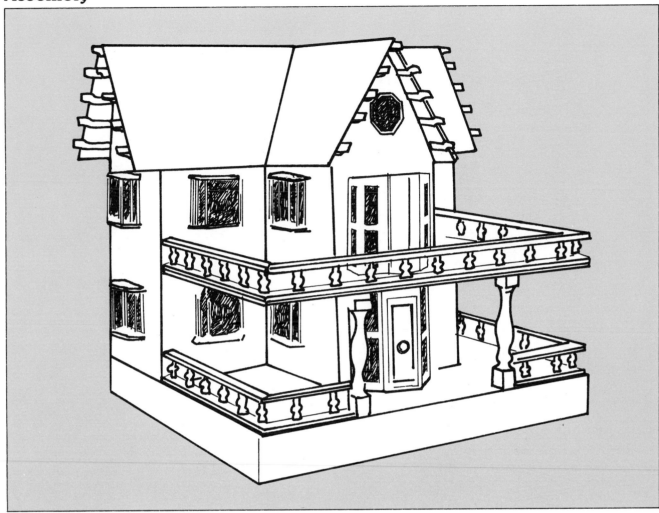

Fig. A. *Mansion dollhouse.*

Consult the assembly diagrams frequently during the construction process to eliminate mistakes.

The Base:

Nail the 2 side base supports (Y) and the front and back base supports (Z) to the base (X). The front and back supports overlap the edges of the side supports.

Outer walls and inner floors:

1. Each of the inner floors (second and third) is attached to the house walls by means of small support strips of ⅜-in. plywood.

2. Cut 28 plywood strips about 4-in. long and ½-in. wide and attach them on the **inside** of each of the 7 outer wall pieces (A, B & C) where indicated on the drawings. (Exact placement is not necessary).

3. Cut 10 strips and nail them on the outside of each of the 5 outer wall pieces A and B. These strips should be 4-in. long also, and should be at the height of the second floor supports. The top of these strips should measure the same height as the 2 front porch posts. Adjust the height of either the porch posts or the balcony supports to match.

4. Nail the outer walls together, overlapping the walls as shown in the top view assembly diagram.

5. Insert the second floor so that it rests on the inner supports and glue and nail it in place.

6. Repeat the same procedure for the third floor.

Attaching the house to the base

1. Cut 6 plywood strips 7-in. long and ½-in. wide, and 2 strips 2-in. long and ½-in. wide.

2. Center 1 strip at the bottom of 6 of the inner walls (B and C). Nail and glue the strip in place to attach the house to the base.

3. Attach the two 2-in. strips to each side of the front door.

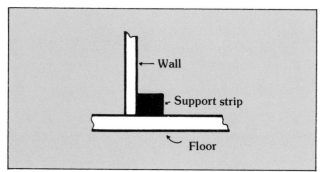

Fig. B. *Inner walls and floor.*

Adding the balcony and roof

1. Glue and nail the balcony to the outer walls. Support the balcony in the front with the wooden posts (or substitute wooden dowel rods). Glue and nail them in place.

2. Glue and nail front roof and back roof to the completed house as shown in the assembly diagram. Attach front roof extensions to the front roof.

3. An optional step at this point is to cover the top of the roof line by cutting narrow strips (or use ¼-in.-diameter wooden dowel rods). Glue and nail in place.

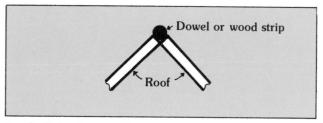

Fig. C. *Optional narrow strips.*

Finishing

1. Assemble, glue and nail windows and doors over openings as shown in the assembly diagram.

2. Beams and railings should be cut to size and glued and nailed as shown on the diagram. Corners may be mitred on railings, or simply cut straight.

OLD-FASHIONED CARS/SPORTS CARS

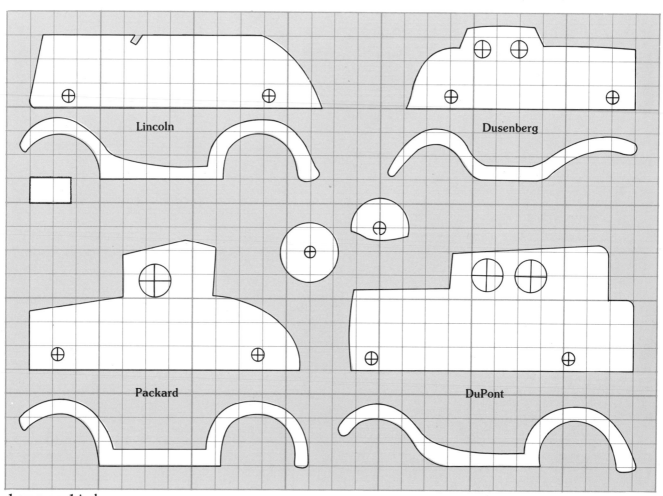

Lincoln

Dusenberg

Packard

DuPont

1 square = 1 inch

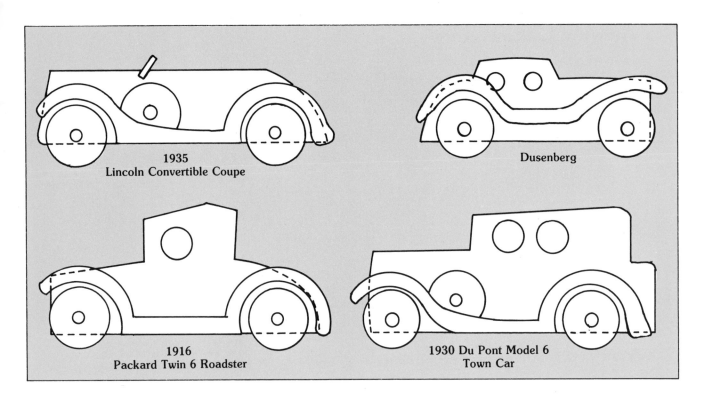

1935
Lincoln Convertible Coupe

Dusenberg

1916
Packard Twin 6 Roadster

1930 Du Pont Model 6
Town Car

Pattern pieces and lumber

Car	Qty.	Pattern pieces	Type of lumber*	Total length	Drill bits	Other
Dusenberg	1	Body	2 × 4	11-in.	¾-in.,	4 metal washers with at
	2	Fenders	1 × 4	22-in.	⁹⁄₁₆-in., ½-in.	least ⁹⁄₁₆-in. center
	4	Lg. wheels	1 × 4	12-in.		hole
	2	Axles	½-in. dowel	8-in.		
Lincoln	1	Body	2 × 4	14-in.	⁹⁄₁₆-in., ½-in.	4 metal washers (same
	2	Fenders	1 × 4	28-in.		as above)
	4	Lg. wheels	1 × 4	12-in.		Optional "person"
	2	Spare tire	1 × 4	6-in.		requires 1-in. diameter
	1	Windshield	¼-in. lumber	2-in.		wood drawer pull (or round finial) for head,
	2	Axles	½-in. dowel	8-in.		and ½-in. wood dowel for neck (1½-in. long)
Packard	1	Body	2 × 4	13-in.	1¼-in.,	4 metal washers (same
	2	Fenders	1 × 4	26-in.	⁹⁄₁₆-in., ½-in.	as above)
	4	Lg. wheels	1 × 4	12-in.		
	2	Axles	½-in. dowel	8-in.		
DuPont	1	Body	2 × 6	14-in.	1¼-in.,	4 metal washers (same
	2	Fenders	1 × 4	28-in.	⁹⁄₁₆-in., ½-in.	as above)
	4	Lg. wheels	1 × 4	12-in.		
	2	Axles	½-in. dowel	8-in.		

* Indicates minimum width.

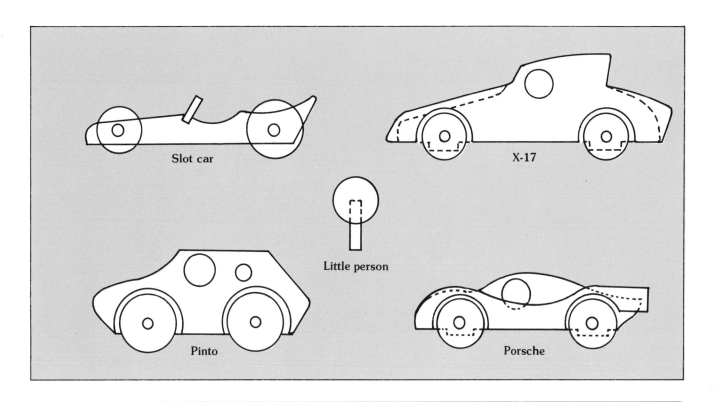

Slot car

X-17

Little person

Pinto

Porsche

Pattern pieces and lumber

Car	Qty.	Pattern piece	Type of lumber*	Total length	Drill bits	Other
Porsche	1	Body	2 × 4	11-in.	1¼-in.,	4 metal washers with at
	2	Fenders	1 × 4	22-in.	9/16-in., ½-in.	least 9/16-in. middle
	4	Sm. wheels	1 × 4	10-in.		holes
	2	Axles	½-in. dowel	8-in.		
X-17	1	Inner body	2 × 6	13-in.	1¼-in.,	4 washers (as above)
	2	Outer body	1 × 6	26-in.	9/16-in., ½-in.	2 optional "little
	4	Sm. wheels	1 × 4	10-in.		person" require 1-in.
	2	Axles	½-in. dowel	8-in.		diameter wood drawer pull (or round finial) for head, ½-in. wood dowel for neck (1½-in. long)
Slot Car	1	Body	2 × 4	12-in.	9/16-in., ½-in.	4 washers (as above)
	1	Windshield	¼-in. lumber	2-in.		1 optional "little person" (as above)
	2	Axles	½-in. dowel	8-in.		
	2	Lg. wheel	1 × 4	6-in.		
	2	Sm. wheel	1 × 4	5-in.		
Pinto	1	Inner body	2 × 4	10-in.	1¼-in.,	4 washers (as above)
	2	Outer body	1 × 4	20-in.	9/16-in., ½-in.	
	4	Lg. wheel	1 × 4	12-in.		
	2	Axles	½-in. dowel	8-in.		

* Indicates minimum width.

Materials

To determine the materials necessary to build each car, consult the chart. In addition to the materials listed in the chart, you will need: a sabre saw (or hand coping saw), scissors, a drill (electric is faster), 2 or 3 sheets each of medium and fine garnet sandpaper, white glue or aliphatic resin (a wood glue), wood clamp or two C-clamps. An optional help is a circle-cutter attachment for a ¼-in. electric drill.

Cutting the pieces

1. Enlarge and cut out individual paper pattern pieces needed for the car you are building. Be sure to use the correct thickness and width of wood (1 × 6, 2 × 4, etc.) as indicated on the chart. To cut 2 fenders (outer bodies) for each car, tape 2 pieces of wood together with masking tape and cut them both out at the same time. Cut the wood carefully along the outer pattern lines.

2. Cut the proper number and size of wheels (listed on the chart). Cut two 4-in. lengths of ½-in. wood dowel rod for each car, which will be the axles.

Drilling and sanding

1. Drill two ⁹/₁₆-in. holes through the car body for the axles where indicated. Drill as straight as possible so the wheels will be even on the finished toy.

2. Drill all window holes with the size drill bit corresponding to the size on the pattern.

3. Drill ½-in. holes through the exact center of all wheels.

4. Thoroughly sand all pieces of wood. Begin with medium sandpaper and finish with fine. Sand until no sharp edges remain.

Assembling

Each car (with the exception of the slot-car) has 3 main body pieces—1 middle piece of 2-in. thick lumber, and 2 outside pieces of 1-in. thick lumber.

1. Wipe a thin coat of glue on each of the 1-in. thick outer pieces on the side which faces the center of the car.

2. Place the glued pieces on each side of the middle body and press in place tightly with your hands.

3. Tightly clamp the assembled car (or place a heavy weight on top) and allow the glue to dry overnight.

Adding the wheels

1. Insert the 4-in. lengths of wood dowel through the axle holes.

2. Slip a washer onto both ends of each axle dowel.

3. Attach the proper size wheels with a spot of glue. Let the glue set overnight.

Adding the little "person" (optional)

To add the driver to your car, first insert the wood dowel into the head. Then drill a ½-in. diameter hole into the top of the car (about ½-in. deep) just behind the windshield slot in the car. Wipe glue on the end of the wood dowel, and insert it in the hole. Allow to dry.

Windshield

Wipe a thin coat of glue along 1 of the long edges of the windshield and press it firmly into the windshield slot. Allow to dry.

Finishing

We left our toys natural wood, but you can stain or paint them if you wish. Be sure to use a non-toxic stain or paint to protect little ones.

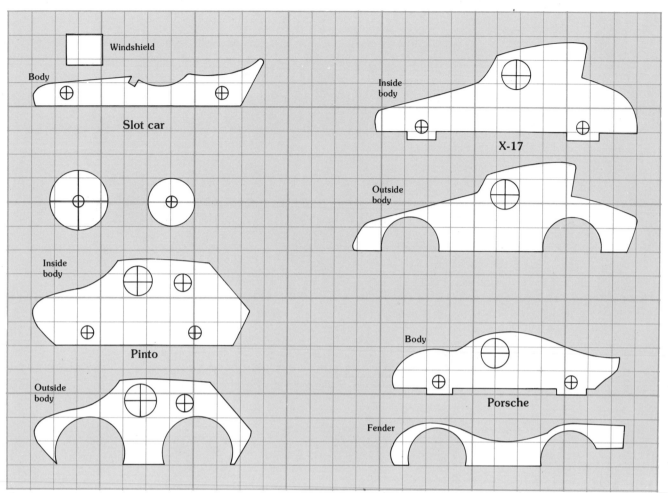

Windshield

Body

Slot car

Inside body

Pinto

Outside body

Inside body

X-17

Outside body

Body

Porsche

Fender

1 square = 1-inch

MY
CRITTERS

Materials

1 ¼-yd. of 36-in.-wide canvas fabric
7 yds. of wide bias binding in your choice of color
Fabric scraps for animals (we used calico and felt)
4 metal rings
Buttons, rick-rack, and yarn scraps for trim
Polyester fiberfill for stuffing the critters

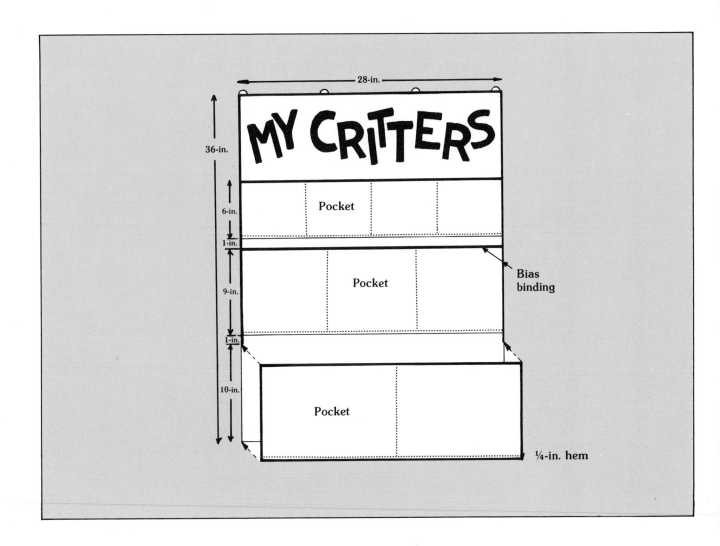

Sewing

The hang-up:

1. Cut 1 main piece 36 × 28-in.

2. Cut 3 strips for pockets to the following dimensions: 28 × 6-in., 28 × 9 ins., and 28 × 10-ins.

3. Cover the top of each strip with bias tape (see illustration).

4. Sew a ¼-in. hem along the bottom of each pocket and pin the pocket in place on the main canvas piece, as shown in the illustration.

5. Sew across the hem of each pocket. Divide each large pocket by sewing from top to bottom through the main piece.

6. Cover all 4 outside raw edges with bias tape. Be sure to include the pocket edges when sewing.

7. Add metal rings to the top for hanging the piece. Simply slip a piece of bias tape through the metal rings, then sew the tape ends to the top back of the hang-up at even intervals.

8. Draw the "My Critters" letters onto felt scraps and cut out. Sew in place. (You can also use iron-on letters sold in craft stores if you prefer.)

1 square = 1 inch

The Critters

1. Enlarge and draw the critter designs onto the right side of the fabric.

2. Place the pattern design on top of another piece of fabric, wrong sides together. Pin the pieces together, and cut them both at the same time, creating a front and back for each critter.

3. Place the same 2 pieces right sides together, and sew along the solid line, leaving an opening large enough to turn and stuff the critter.

4. Turn the critter right side out, stuff with polyester fiberfill, and blind-stitch the opening shut.

5. Wings and ears, shown in place, should be cut out of felt and sewn on the stuffed critter.

6. Add buttons for eyes and rick-rack and yarn for trim, as shown in the picture.